Learn Windows 10 in 1 Quick Week

Beginner to Pro

The Ultimate User Guide for Learning Windows 10 Visually!

By Bob Roberts

Windows 10 is a trademark of Microsoft corporation. *Learn in 1 Quick Week* is a trademark of Learn It The Quick Way Ltd. All other trademarks are the property of their respective owners.

Cover Design: Creative Arts Ltd.
Development Editors: Lisa Johnston, Mark Fielding
Technical Editors: Content Masters
Proofreaders: John Morgan, Linda Rice, Todd Spencer

About the Author

Bob Roberts has an extensive background in Windows training, having taught millions through his written words and classroom instruction during the past twenty-plus years. Though Windows users throughout the world have read Bob's work, attended his training seminars and followed his expert advice, this is his first book published as "Bob Roberts." Bob continues to work with Microsoft Corporation on a variety of Windows-related projects, including training courses and documentation.

Table of Contents

Day 1

Ready. Set. Go Windows 10

Day 1.
Ready. Set. Go Windows 10

Lesson Notes: The lessons in Day 1 teach you about the new features of Windows and how they can help you.

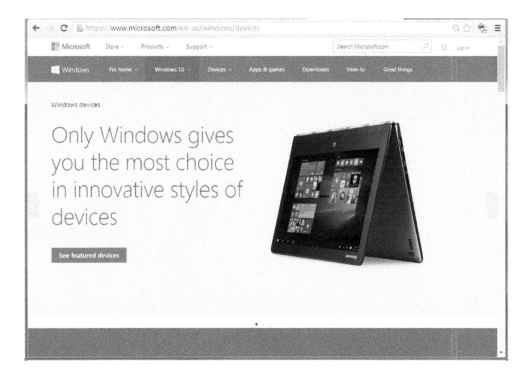

Windows 10 provides an immersive experience unlike any previous release of the operating system. Not only do many new features and advanced options differentiate it from previous releases, but the operating system is designed to run more quickly and efficiently.

When you first start working with Windows 10, you'll notice that it combines many of the best features of Windows 7 and Windows 8.1.

From Windows 7, you get many core features and options that users love, including the traditional Start Menu. From Windows 8.1, you get a consistent user interface across mobile and desktop devices.

Windows 10 also has many new features that are exclusive to the operating system and haven't been available previously.

What's In This Book...

If you're reading this book, you likely have recently installed Windows 10 on your computer or are considering installing Windows 10 and want to learn more about the operating system beforehand. You are also likely to be looking for quick answers and quick solutions to help you make the transition to this new operating system.

Learn Windows 10 in 1 Quick Week is designed for both beginners and professional users. In this book, you will get advice and guidance on working with the operating system and unlocking powerful features, hidden options, and more. Some of the topics covered in this book include:

- Tips and tricks for getting the most from Windows 10
- Guidance on navigating the Start Menu, Settings, Accounts
- Insights on working with the new File Explorer and file system
- Advice on personalizing Windows 10 and managing the desktop
- Steps for optimizing your system
- Much, much more!

Not only is this book designed to be used with all editions of Windows, it's also designed to be used whether you will use Windows 10 on a desktop, laptop or tablet. The key reason to purchase this book is that it'll help you get the most out of Windows 10 in less time and with less fuss. This book illustrates fundamental tips and tricks in plain language, with clear, simple guidance. Using the insights in this book to simplify tasks and get more done in less time is what *Learn in 1 Quick Week*™ books are all about!

Learn Windows 10 in 1 Quick Week is designed to be read in seven sessions, whether those sessions occur over different or consecutive days is entirely up to you. The early sessions are designed to be the easiest and are meant to get you thinking about Windows 10 and what your options are. The later sessions explore key features and options of the operating system. In all, the seven sessions provide guidance on performing nearly 100 fundamental tasks.

If you follow a day-by-day plan, here's an overview of each day:

Day 1 – Teaches you about this book and about the new features and editions of Windows 10.

Day 2 – Provides a jump start that teaches you how to about key features of Windows 10.

Day 3 – Examines features and options that can help you stay connected and use Windows 10 to its fullest potential.

Day 4 – Teaches you about connected accounts, providing guidance on why and how you can use them.

Day 5 – Provides advice and instruction on getting and using apps so you can boost your productivity and increase efficiency when you work with Windows 10.

Day 6 – Examines advanced options for working with apps.

Day 7 – Teaches you about customizing the look and feel of Windows so you can personalize your working space.

Each day plan to spend up to one hour with the text, so set aside this time and block it out for learning Windows 10. During each session, you'll ideally take notes, make highlights and work to understand the ideas presented. As you read the individual lessons, be sure to practice the techniques you've learned.

> **TIP**: Throughout this book, where I use click, right-click, and double-click, you can use the touch equivalents of tap, press-and-hold, and double-tap.

Finally, don't forget this book is intended as a quick reference too. Whenever you have a question about any task this book covers, simply open the book, look up the task and follow the step-by-step instructions. Whether you are using the printed book or reading an ebook on a device, you can open the book and reference it as you work.

Ready to begin your Windows 10 journey? Keep reading...

Meet the New Windows

Windows 10 is the newest operating system from Microsoft. The operating system is offered as a free upgrade for certain users, including those with:

- Qualified Windows 7 devices
- Qualified Windows 8.1 devices

Windows 10 also comes preinstalled on new devices, including desktops, laptops and tablets. Other users and businesses must purchase Windows 10.

If you haven't installed Windows 10 yet, find out if you qualify for a free upgrade by visiting http://www.microsoft.com/en-us/windows/windows-10-upgrade.

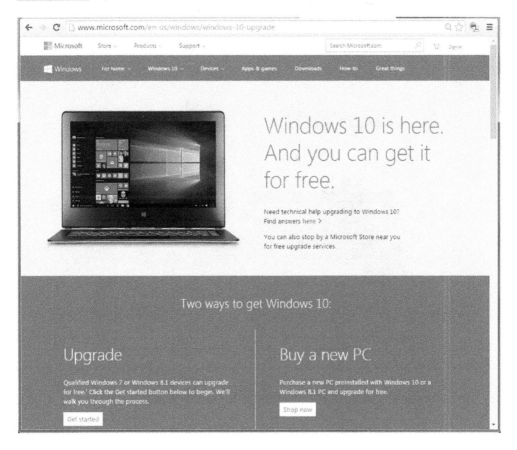

Windows 10 was officially released on July 29, 2015, and is supposedly, the last version of Windows—though it's hard to say whether that's really true or simply a marketing tactic. More likely, it's the last version of Windows that will be delivered as a software product purchased through stores—with future releases of the operating system coming directly from Microsoft.

This latest version of Windows is optimized for both touch-screen and the traditional mouse-and-keyboard interfaces. The operating system has many features of both Windows 7 and Windows 8.1 and also brings back the Start Menu, though tablet users may continue to see a Start screen whenever they use Tablet mode.

NOTE: Windows 7, Windows 8 and Windows 8.1 were previous releases of the Windows operating system with Windows 8.1 being an update to the original Windows 8 release. Rather than referring to Windows 8/8.1 throughout this book, I simply refer to Windows 8.1.

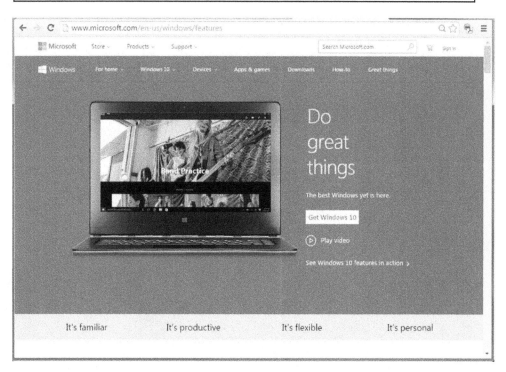

The minimum hardware requirements for using Windows 10 are:

- 1 gigahertz (GHz) or faster processor (or a System on a Chip (SoC) device, such as a Windows Phone)
- 1 gigabyte (GB) of RAM for 32-bit systems, 2 GB of RAM for 64-bit systems
- 16 GB of disk space for 32-bit systems, 20 GB of disk space for 64-bit systems
- Graphics card with DirectX 9 or later with WDDM 1.0 or later drivers

New features in Windows 10 include:

- Fast start up that can use Hyperboot and Instant Go to quickly resume
- Microsoft Edge browser for a streamlined web browsing experience
- Cortana, a digital assistant, to help get things done quickly using your voice
- Windows Hello, a security feature that allows login with a look or a touch (on systems with cameras, fingerprint readers and other compliant hardware)
- Virtual Desktop System for creating virtual desktops and seeing open tasks in a single view.
- Continuum which allows you to switch easily and instantly between desktop and tablet mode.
- OneDrive which allows you to easily store documents and photos in the cloud and then access those documents and photos anywhere you can use your account.
- Windows Store for purchasing apps, movies, music, games and more.
- Xbox app for streaming games from your Xbox to your Windows 10 device and staying connected to the Xbox Live community.

Apps That Go Where You Go

Universal apps are a key benefit of Windows 10 that you may not be familiar with. As the name implies, universal apps are apps that run across various types of devices seamlessly, from desktops to tablets, smartphones and even Xbox One devices.

Many universal apps are installed on Windows 10 devices out of the box. These apps are available via the Start Menu, as shown in the preceding figure, and include:

- Calendar—a built-in calendar app that allows you to create events and get reminders for appointments.

- Mail—a built-in mail program that you can use to connect and access all your email in one place.
- Microsoft Edge—a web browser with a streamlined interface that allows you to easily add notes to your favorite web pages.
- Photos—a digital collection of all your photos that allows you to create photo albums and share your pictures across devices.
- Weather—a handy weather app that allows you to quickly view the current weather and get weather forecasts
- Groove Music—a music app that puts all your digital music in one place and provides quick access to the music available in the Windows Store.
- Movies & TV—a video player that replaces Windows Media Player and lets you watch movies, television shows and digital videos.
- Maps—a map tool for getting directions and learning about nearby restaurants, stores, coffee houses and more.
- News—a news app for getting local, national and world news.

Many other apps are available for download or purchase in the Windows Store. Anyone familiar with the Google Play or Apple iTunes store knows what the Windows Store is all about.

The Windows Store is where you go to purchase apps, games, music, movies and more. And visiting the Windows Store is as simple as clicking **Store** on the Start Menu.

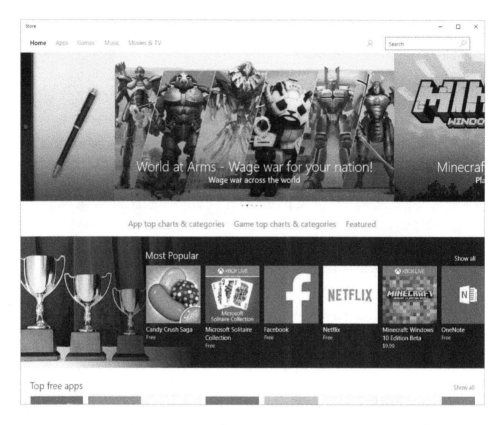

Because store apps are universal apps, any app you use on one device can also be made available on your other devices. Here's how it works:

1. You download or purchase an app in the Windows store using your account.
2. When you sign in to that same account on another device, the app is available for download and install on that device too.
3. If you create files in the app and store the files in OneDrive (the free cloud service for saving files mentioned earlier), those files will be available too.

How cool is that? It's okay, you don't have to answer the question by screaming "Holy sh*t!" out loud (unless you want to).

Settings That Go Where You Go

Unified settings are another key benefit of Windows 10 that you may not be familiar with. As the name implies, unified settings allow you to customize certain aspects of the operating system and have those same settings whenever you log in to your account on any device.

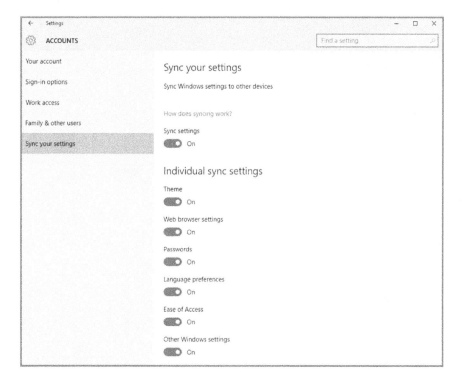

Unified settings rely on the Sync Settings option being enabled, which it is by default. Here's how it works:

1. You log in to your device with your account and personalize Windows and the Edge browser.
2. When you sign in to that same account on another device, the settings are used automatically. This means your favorite colors, account picture, browser favorites and much more will all be there without you having to do anything!

Don't worry, I'll talk more about settings and sync later. For now though, just keep in mind that you can do this.

Virtual Assistance When You Need It

Personal digital assistants are in vogue. Apple has Siri. Google has Google Now. Microsoft has Cortana.

Cortana is designed to provide help and guidance and can be activated in several different ways:

- Cortana can be made available for any time you search the web or Windows.

- Cortana can be used to give you time- and location-based reminders.
- Cortana can also be used to create appointments, set alerts and more.

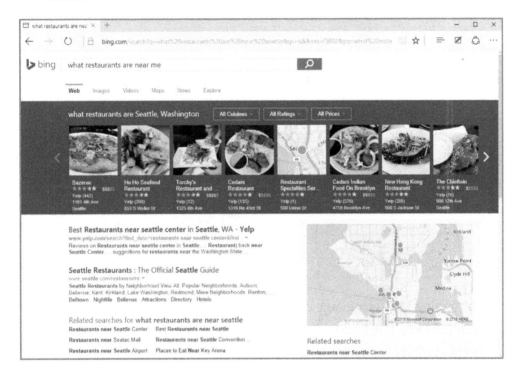

You can ask Cortana questions. For example, you can ask "What restaurants are near me" or "What coffee shops are near me." Cortana will use location information to determine what restaurants or coffee shops are nearby and display information about them. If you say "show my recent photos" or "find my recent word documents," Cortana will search your account for those types of files and display them.

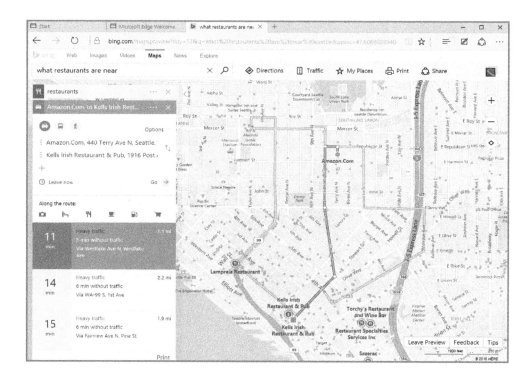

Cortana's natural language abilities are the key to how digital assistance works. As you talk to Cortana, the program learns your voice and gets better at understanding you.

Streamlined Browsing with Microsoft Edge

Microsoft Edge replaces Internet Explorer as the default browser in Windows 10. The Edge browser provides a streamlined browsing experience that gets rid of much of the windows frame and interface to let you see more of what you want to see—namely the websites you are visiting.

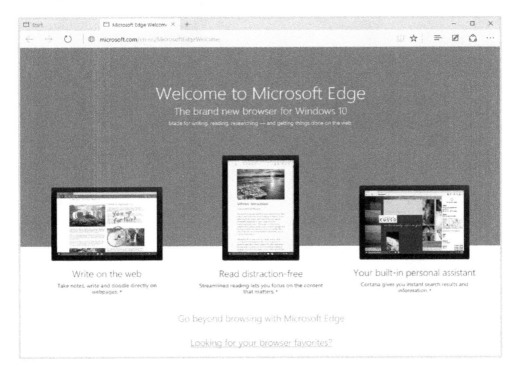

Edge also gets rid of legacy technologies like ActiveX and adds extensions that are more secure and current with the times, including integration with OneDrive and Cortana. Although Edge has many new features, a few that you may use the most are:

- Reading View—A streamlined reading experience that fills the screen and makes it easier to read without distractions.
- Reading List—An enhanced bookmarking feature that lets you save articles or other content that you want to read later.

- Web Note—A notation tool that allows you to take notes, write or doodle directly on web pages and then see those annotations any time you visit the web page.

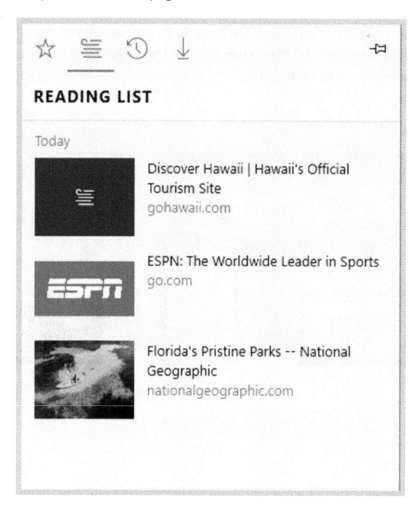

Just because Edge has replaced Internet Explorer as the default browser doesn't mean Internet Explorer isn't available or hasn't been updated. Windows 10 still includes Internet Explorer and the browser can be used for those times when you need access to legacy features such as ActiveX or simply anytime you want to use this popular browser. Internet Explorer version 11, IE 11, is what is available with the original release of Windows 10.

Internet Explorer 11 is an improved version of the original web browser that's been in Windows for many years. Although IE 11 has a streamlined interface similar to Microsoft Edge, IE 11 doesn't have the same features as Edge. With IE 11, you can't write on web pages or get instant search results with Cortana. There isn't a reading list or a Reading View either. That said, as the figure that follows shows, web pages opened in IE 11 will look substantially similar to those opened in Microsoft Edge.

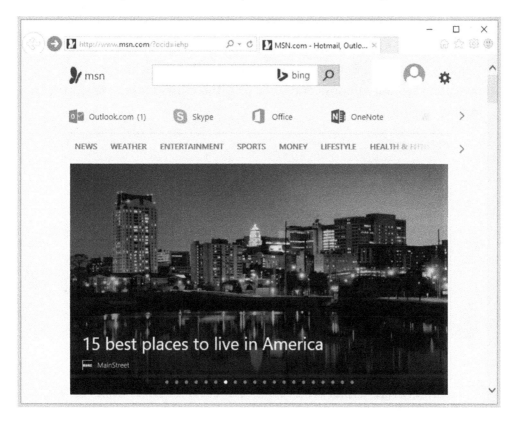

Windows 10 Editions

Like ice cream, Windows 10 comes in different flavors. Each of which is tailored to the needs of different users. You also can compare editions to find the one that's right for you by visiting http://www.microsoft.com/en-us/WindowsForBusiness/Compare.

Meet Windows 10 Home Edition

Windows 10 Home Edition is designed for end-users who use the operating system at home and need only the core essential features. This means you get:

- Continuum
- Cortana

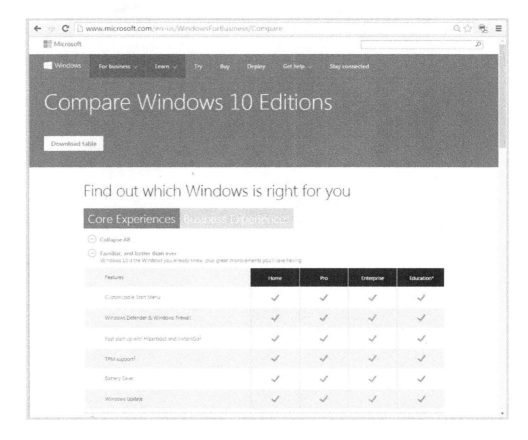

- Microsoft Edge
- Unified settings
- Universal apps
- Virtual Desktop System
- Windows Hello
- More...

Windows 10 Home Edition replaces Windows 7 Home Basic and Windows 7 Home Premium as well as the basic editions for Windows 8.1. The Home Edition supports a maximum of 4 GB RAM on 32-bit systems and 128 GB RAM on 64-bit systems.

> **TIP**: If you have a Home edition of Windows 7 or Windows 8.1, you must upgrade to Windows 10 Home Edition. You can't upgrade to other editions.

Meet Windows 10 Pro Edition

Windows 10 Pro Edition is designed for professionals who use the operating system at work and need extra features for enhanced security, joining domains and connecting to workplaces. This means you get all the features of the Home Edition plus:

- Assigned Access
- BitLocker Drive Encryption
- Client Hyper-V
- Domain Join & Azure Directory Join
- Enterprise Data Protection
- Group Policy Management
- Remote Desktop
- Windows Store for Business
- Windows Update for Business
- More...

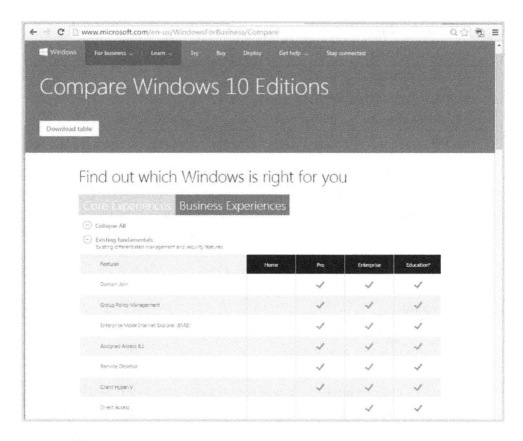

Windows 10 Pro is optimized for those who work in small and medium-sized businesses and can also be used by those who work from home and need to connect to workplaces. Windows 10 Pro replaces Windows 7 Professional and Windows 7 Ultimate as well as the pro editions for Windows 8.1. The Pro Edition supports a maximum of 4 GB RAM on 32-bit systems and 512 GB RAM on 64-bit systems.

> **TIP**: If you have a pro edition of Windows 7 or Windows 8.1, you must upgrade to Windows 10 Pro. You can't upgrade to Windows 10 Home or Enterprise Edition.

Meet Windows 10 Enterprise & Education Editions

Windows 10 Enterprise Edition is designed for professionals who use the operating system in enterprise business settings and large offices. With the Enterprise Edition, you get all the features of Home and Pro plus the extra features needed for deploying and managing Windows 10 on a large scale, including:

- App Locker
- BranchCache
- Direct Access
- Credential Guard
- Device Guard
- Long Term Servicing Branch of Windows 10
- Windows To Go
- More...

Windows 10 Enterprise replaces Windows 7 Enterprise as well as the enterprise edition for Windows 8.1. The Enterprise Edition supports a maximum of 4 GB RAM on 32-bit systems and 512 GB RAM on 64-bit systems.

> **TIP**: If you have an Enterprise edition of Windows 7 or Windows 8.1, you must upgrade to Windows 10 Enterprise Edition. You can't upgrade to the Home or Pro editions.

Meet Windows 10 Education Edition

Windows 10 Education Edition is meant for use by students and those in academia, such as university faculty and professors. This edition has the same features as the Enterprise Edition.

This means you get all the features of Home and Pro plus extra features needed for deploying and managing Windows 10 throughout educational organizations, including:

- App Locker
- BranchCache
- Direct Access
- Credential Guard
- Device Guard
- Windows To Go
- More...

Windows 10 Education replaces Windows 7 Education as well as the education edition for Windows 8.1. The Education Edition supports a maximum of 4 GB RAM on 32-bit systems and 512 GB RAM on 64-bit systems.

> **TIP**: If you have an Education edition of Windows 7 or Windows 8.1, you must upgrade to Windows 10 Education Edition. You can't upgrade to the Home, Pro or Enterprise editions.

Meet Windows 10 Mobile Editions

Windows 10 comes in two mobile versions:

- Windows 10 Mobile Edition
- Windows 10 Mobile Enterprise Edition

Windows 10 Mobile Edition is designed for use on small personal devices that use touch interfaces, such as smartphones and small tablet PCs. The Mobile Edition supports:

- Continuum for Phone
- Touch-optimized Office
- Universal apps
- Unified settings
- More...

Windows 10 Mobile Enterprise Edition is designed for use on small personal devices that are connected to enterprises. Anyone who uses personal smartphones and small tablet PCs at work can use this edition to get enterprise enhancements for security, management and more.

Meet Windows 10 Internet of Things Editions

If you thought the six flavors of Windows 10 was all that was available, think again. Windows 10 is also available in a variety of other editions, including:

- Windows 10 Internet of Things for Industry Devices
- Windows 10 Internet of Things for Mobile Devices

- Windows 10 Internet of Things for Small Devices

These editions are designed for devices used in a variety of home, business and industrial settings and include:

- Desktop Shell for core functionality
- Win32 Apps, Universal Apps and drivers

Although you may find Windows 10 Internet of Things for Small Devices in home appliances and Windows 10 Internet of Things for Mobile Devices in small mobile gadgets and accessories, such as smart watches, you likely won't encounter Windows 10 Internet of Things for Industry Devices unless you work in a light or heavy industry setting.

Windows 10 coffee pot anyone?

Where to Next...

Now that you've learned about know about Windows features and editions, you're ready to begin using Windows 10. *Learn Windows 10 in 1 Quick Week* next looks at the Start Menu, desktop and taskbar. Keep in mind, however, you aren't limited to the options you can find on Start, the desktop or the taskbar—and this book will help you unlock the options, features and secrets of the operating system.

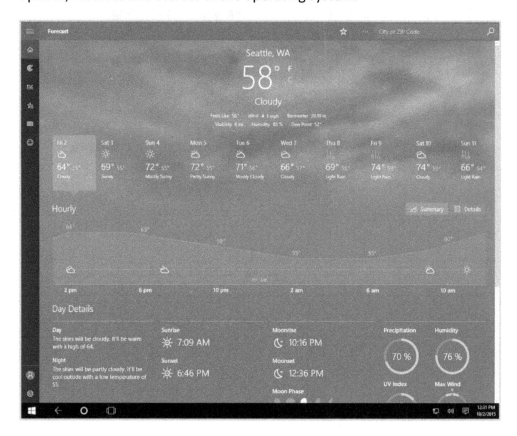

In the lessons that follow, you will find clear, simple guidance that allows you to get to know the basic features of Windows 10. You'll also learn tips and tricks that will help you quickly master the new options and interfaces. A key goal of this book is to help anyone—beginners and pros alike—get the most out of the operating system while increasing efficiency and productivity.

Day 2

Windows 10 Jump Start

Day 2.
Windows 10 Jump Start

Lesson Notes: To get started with Windows 10, you need to sign in and explore the desktop and the menu system. You also need to learn desktop options.

If you upgraded to Windows 10 from Windows 7, the Windows 10 desktop may look a little different than you're used to—and that's because a lot has changed. To avoid getting confused as you try to find your way around, you need to take a few moments to learn where things are on the new desktop. You also need to learn about the new Start menu (or Start screen if you're using a tablet PC in tablet mode).

Getting Signed In

Windows 10 has a new sign in process that allows you to use new ways to access Windows on your device. If your account is the only one on your device and your device doesn't have secure login enabled, you are signed in automatically each time you use your device. Otherwise, you'll need to log in to access your device.

Lock Screen

Whenever you start or wake your device, you'll see a Lock screen. This screen is also displayed when you lock your device. Simply tap or click to go the login screen (or directly to the desktop, if applicable).

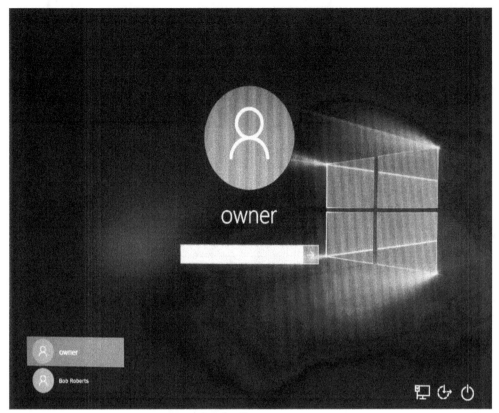

Login Screen

If the device has multiple users, click your account name in the lower left corner of the screen and then provide the required authorization information.

The authorization information required for login can take many forms, but typically includes specifying a:

- Password—A string of upper and lowercase letters, numbers and special characters.
- Pin—A sequence of numbers, usually four or more.
- Picture password—a password drawn on the screen by a series of finger or mouse movements.

If your Windows 10 device has capable hardware, you may also be able to use the following for log in:

- Fingerprint—a touch of your finger to the biometric fingerprint scanner.
- Face scan—a camera on your device can scan your face.

Thus, the basic steps to login are:

1. Tap or click on the Lock screen to access the Login screen.
2. Click your account, if needed.
3. Type your password or PIN.

4. Click the login button ( ).

TIP: Click the **Reveal** ( ) icon to see the password or PIN you typed.

Exploring the New Desktop

In Windows 10, Microsoft moved the furniture around and provided new options on the desktop. Most of these new options are available on the taskbar—the bar shown by default at the bottom of the desktop.

The Taskbar

The taskbar has many options. Each option has a specific purpose that will be discussed next. Icons for programs you have open are added to the taskbar automatically. This makes it easier to work with programs. For example, you can use the program icons to switch from one program to another if you have more than one running at a time.

Start Button

You use the Start button to display the Start menu, which in turn allows you to open apps and access features of the operating system.

Search Box with Cortana

The Search box allows you to search for items on your Windows devices or on the web. When Cortana is enabled, the Search box looks as shown above, letting you know you can use your voice to ask Cortana questions. Regardless of whether Cortana is enabled, you can always type text in the Search box to search as well.

Taskbar Icons

The taskbar icons let you use some Windows features with just a tap or a click.

Notification Area

As the name implies, the Notification area is where Windows notifies you about things that are happening on your Windows device. Windows displays notifications for various reasons, including when there are problems or issues you should be aware of.

Time and Date

The taskbar always displays the time and date. If you tap or click the time, you'll see the full calendar for the current month.

11:19:16 AM

Friday, October 02, 2015

October 2015

Su	Mo	Tu	We	Th	Fr	Sa
27	28	29	30	1	2	3
4	5	6	7	8	9	10
11	12	13	14	15	16	17
18	19	20	21	22	23	24
25	26	27	28	29	30	31
1	2	3	4	5	6	7

Date and time settings

TIP: While you are viewing the calendar, click **Date And Time Settings** to view more information about the time and date settings, such as the current time zone.

Exploring the New Start

Yes, the Start menu is back in Windows 10 (after being replaced in Windows 8.1). That doesn't mean it's the same Start you may be used to. Start has in fact changed a lot.

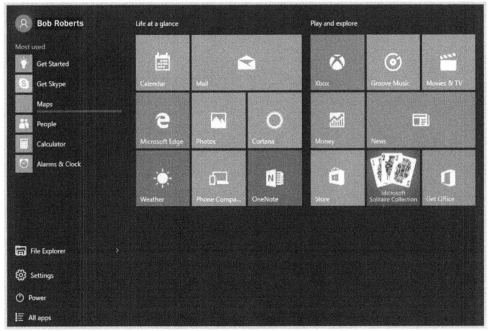

The New Start Menu

Start is divided into two several areas:

- Information and options
- Tiles for apps

Name of Current User

On the left, you have information and options beginning with the name of the currently logged in user. If you click the user name, you can get additional options.

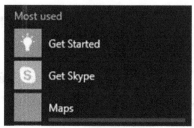
Most Used Apps

Below the user name is a list of the most used apps. Click an app to open it.

Windows Options

In the lower left corner, you have options that allow you to work with Windows 10:

- File Explorer—Opens the File Explorer, which has replaced Windows Explorer as the go to tool for working with files and folders.
- Settings—Opens the Settings app, which allows you to configure many Windows settings, though Control Panel is still used to configure many other settings.
- Power—Displays power options for managing the power state of your device.
- All Apps—Opens the All Apps view on the Start menu so you can find apps that are installed and available for your use.

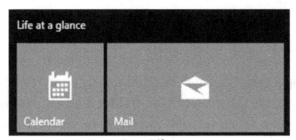

App Tiles

On the right, you have tiles for apps. Tiles replace the traditional program icons used in earlier releases of Windows. Clicking a tile launches the related program.

TIP: Windows 10 has two types of tiles: live tiles and regular tiles. Live tiles display updates and recent information. For example, the tile for the Weather app displays information about current weather without you having to start the app.

Exploring the Tablet Screen

If you are using a tablet or small device, such as a smart phone, Windows 10 will automatically use tablet mode. Tablet mode is designed to make it easier to work with touch screens, especially on small devices.

In tablet mode, Windows 10 works different from the way it works in standard mode. When you log in, you see the Tablet screen by default.

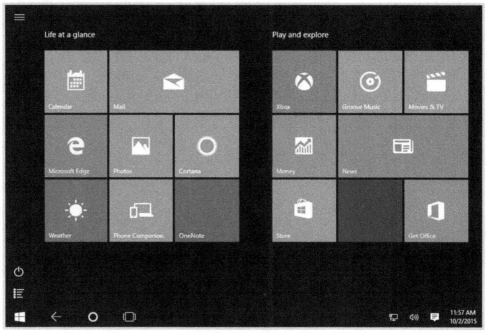

Tablet Screen

The Tablet screen combines features of the Start and desktop. As with Start, tiles are displayed and clicking a tile launches the related program.

Menu Button

To get the full Start options, you must click the Menu button, which is in the upper left corner of the screen. You'll then see user information, most used apps, and Windows options.

Back Button

In tablet mode, each app you open is displayed full screen. One way to switch apps is to use the Back button. Click Back to return either to the previous app screen or to the Start screen.

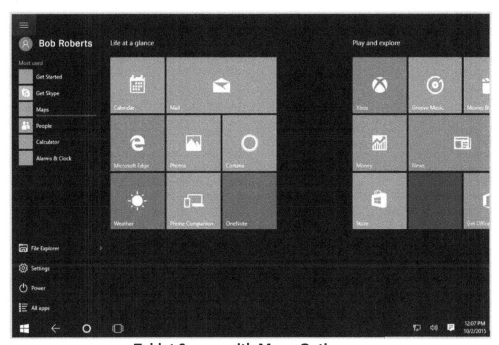

Tablet Screen with Menu Options

As shown in the figure above, the menu options displayed are similar to when you are using Windows 10 with Tablet mode turned off. To hide the additional options, simply click the Menu button again.

Notifications Button

TIP: To turn Tablet mode on or off, click the Notifications button and then click Tablet Mode.

Using Multiple Desktops

Your desktop is where you go to work with your apps. When you open apps, their windows are displayed on the desktop. In earlier releases of Windows, you had a single desktop. Now thanks to the Virtual Desktop System in Windows 10, you can create multiple desktops and easily switch between them.

To add a virtual desktop:

1. Click the **Task View** () button on the taskbar.
2. Click **New Desktop**.

After Windows creates the new desktop, your original desktop is shown as Desktop 1 and the new desktop is shown as Desktop 2. If you create another desktop, that desktop will be shown as Desktop 3, and so on.

> **TIP**: Each virtual desktop is a space where you can open and arrange app windows. At work, you could have one virtual desktop space for each project you are working on. At home, you could have one virtual desktop when you are for working from home and one virtual desktop for when you are relaxing and connecting with friends on social media.

To switch from one desktop to another:

1. Click the **Task View** ( ) button on the taskbar to display a preview of the available desktops.
2. Click the desktop you want to use.

Windows switches to the desktop you selected and displays the windows opened on this desktop. If you start new apps, those apps open on the new desktop.

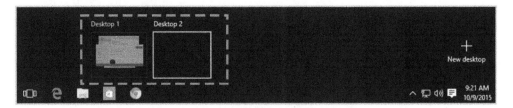

To close a desktop:

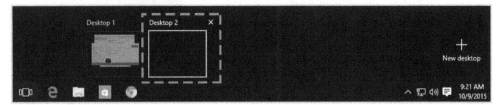

1. Click the **Task View** (⬚) button on the taskbar to display a preview of the available desktops.
2. Move the mouse pointer over the desktop you want to close.
3. Click **Close** (✕).

Searching Windows & the Web

Plain language search is one of the most important connected features of Windows 10. These built-in search features make it easier to find apps, settings, and documents on your device, as well as websites on the Internet. To use the search feature, all you need to do is enter a question or keyword in the Search box.

Windows provides other ways to search as well, including using File Explorer, Microsoft Edge and Internet Explorer—all of which have their own search boxes. When you search using File Explorer, you search for documents and data files on your device. When you search using a web browser, such as Microsoft Edge, you search websites on the Internet.

To perform a basic search:

1. Click in the Search box and type your question or keywords.

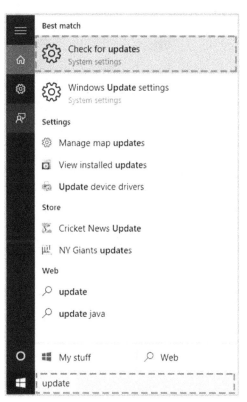

> TIP: If the Search box isn't displayed on the taskbar, click **Start** and then type your search text in the Search box.

2. Windows displays the top matches with names that include your search text. The best matches are shown first. Other results are organized by category, such as whether a result is a system setting, in the Windows Store or from a website.

3. Click the item you want and Windows opens the related app, setting, document or website.

If you get too many results or simply can't find the item you are looking for, you may need to modify the search results so that you only see the type of results you are interested in. For example, it may be helpful to only see items from your device or only items from the Web.

To perform an advanced or modified search:

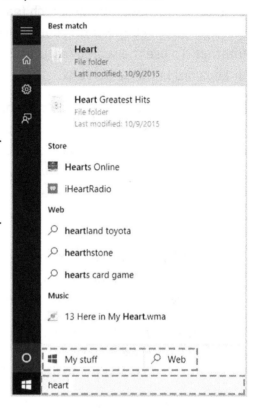

1. Click in the Search box and type your question or keywords.

> **TIP**: If the Search box isn't displayed on the taskbar, click **Start** and then type your search text in the Search box.

2. Windows displays the top matches with names that include your search text. If you see the item you want, click it and skip the remaining steps. Otherwise, continue this procedure.

3. To streamline the results, click **My Stuff** to only see results from your device or click **Web** to only see results from the Web.

4. By default, results are sorted by Most Relevant. To sort results by Most Recent, click in the **Sort** list and then select **Most Recent**.
5. By default, results of all types are shown. To show only a specific type of result, such as Apps, Settings or Documents, click in the **Show** list and then select the item type.
6. If there are too many similar items, only a subset of the items is shown. Click the **See All** option to display all of the items.
7. Click the item you want and Windows opens the related app, setting, document or website.

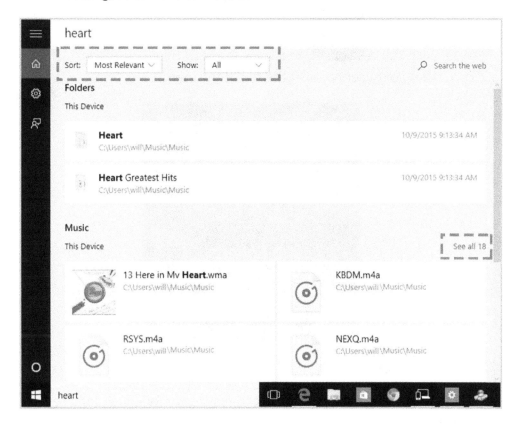

Locking Your Screen

When you step away from your computer or put away your device, you may want to lock the screen to prevent others from accessing your device.

To lock your screen:

1. Click **Start** () to display the Start menu.
2. Click your user name at the top of the menu.

3. Click **Lock**.

TIP: You can also lock your screen by pressing the Windows logo key

(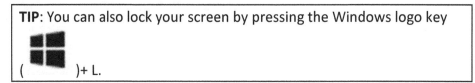)+ L.

You can also configure your device to automatically turn off the screen after it has been idle for a specified amount of time. To configure the screen to turn off automatically:

1. Click **Start** (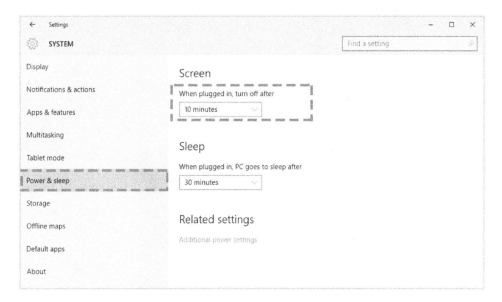) to display the Start menu.

2. Click **Settings** ( ) to open the Settings app.
3. Click **System**, then click **Power & Sleep**.

Settings		– □ ×
⚙ SYSTEM		Find a setting 🔎
Display	**Screen**	
Notifications & actions	When plugged in, turn off after	
Apps & features	10 minutes ∨	
Multitasking		
Tablet mode	**Sleep**	
	When plugged in, PC goes to sleep after	
Power & sleep	30 minutes ∨	
Storage		
Offline maps	**Related settings**	
Default apps	Additional power settings	
About		

4. Under **Screen**, use the **When Plugged In, Turn Off After** list to specify the number of minutes of idle time before Windows turns off the display when running on A/C power.
5. If available, use the **On Battery, Turn Off After** list under the **Screen** heading to specify the number of minutes of idle time before Windows turns off the display when running on battery power.

Signing Out & Switching Users

If you share your device with other users, you may want to sign out when you are done using Windows. When you sign out, Windows closes all the open apps and frees the memory and other resources the apps were using. Once you've signed out, a different user can then sign in.

To sign out:

1. Click **Start** () to display the Start menu.
2. Click your user name at the top of the menu.

3. Click **Sign Out**.

If you want to save your workspace, you can switch users instead of signing out. When you switch users, Windows keeps a snapshot of all your open windows and documents and allows you to resume your work next time you log in.

To switch users:

1. Click **Start** (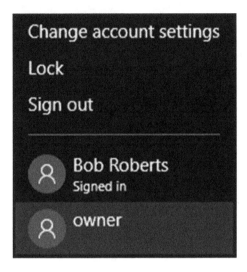) to display the Start menu.
2. Click your user name at the top of the menu.

Change account settings

Lock

Sign out

Bob Roberts
Signed in

owner

3. Click the account of the user you are switching to.
4. This user can then login and begin working.

TIP: Before switching users, make sure you save your documents and other work. This way your work will be preserved if the other user needs to shut down or restart the device.

Day 3

Staying Connected with Windows 10

Day 3.
Staying Connected with Windows 10

Lesson Notes: Now that you know how to get around the interface, let's look at how you can start using Windows 10.

Staying connected with Windows 10 means different things to different people. In this lesson, it means:

- Managing your device's power states
- Connecting your smart phone to Windows 10
- Using key connected features of Windows 10
- Connecting to wireless networks

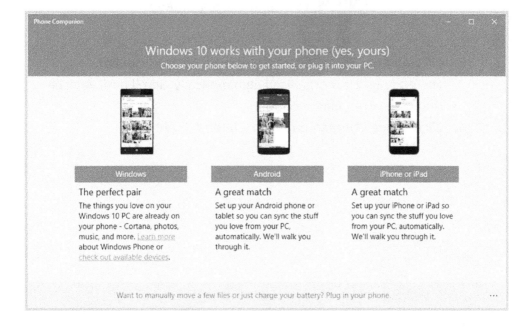

Using Phone Companion

Windows 10 includes Phone Companion as a standard app. Phone Companion works with any compatible phone, allowing you to easily transfer documents, photos, music, email and more between your smart phone and your PC. Once you set up Phone Companion, selected data is transferred automatically whenever you plug your phone into your computer. Plugging your phone into your computer also allows you to charge your phone.

To start Phone Companion:

1. Click **Start** ( ) to display the Start menu.

2. Click **All Apps** ( ) to display the All Apps sidebar.
3. The All Apps list is organized alphabetically. Scroll until you see the Phone Companion option.
4. Click **Phone Companion** to launch the related app.

To set up phone companion:

1. After following steps 1-4 for starting Phone Companion, plug your phone into your PC.
2. Click one of the options provided to specify whether you are using a Windows phone, an Android phone, iPhone or iPad.
3. Use the options provided to get guided assistance for automatically transferring various types of data between your smart phone and Windows PC.

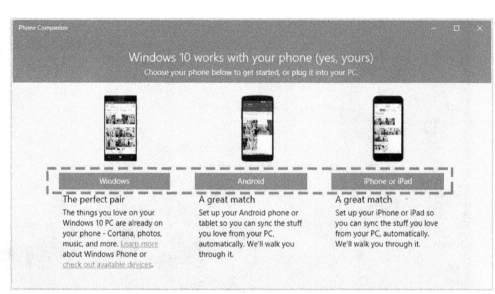

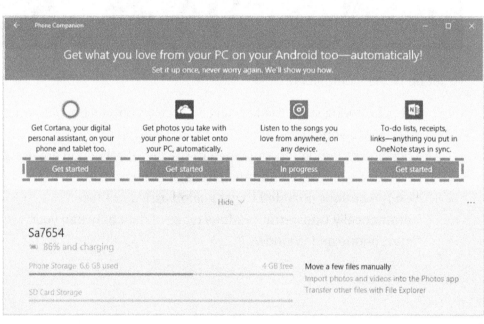

Once you've connected your phone to your PC, you also can use File Explorer to move some types of files. To access the data on your phone using File Explorer:

1. Click **File Explorer** () on the taskbar.

2. Click **This PC** (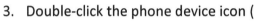).

3. Double-click the phone device icon (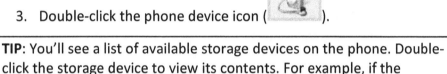).

TIP: You'll see a list of available storage devices on the phone. Double-click the storage device to view its contents. For example, if the storage device is named Phone, double-click **Phone** to access all the data in this storage area of your phone.

Managing System Time

As many operating system features depend on your device's system clock being accurate, Windows 10:

- Automatically synchronizes the system time with world time.
- Adjusts for daylight saving time (in the U.S. and elsewhere as applicable).
- Manages the time zone as per your selection during initial setup.

To ensure Windows is able to sync your device's clock with world time, you must periodically connect to the Internet. Thus, if the system time on your device isn't accurate, you can resolve this simply by connecting to the Internet and staying connected long enough for Windows to sync the clock.

Other clock settings won't necessarily change automatically. If you are physically in a different time zone or your device has an incorrect time zone setting, you typically will need to set the time zone manually when you are using a desktop, laptop or tablet PC. Other times, such as when you have a smart phone or small tablet running a mobile edition of Windows 10, the device may be able to update its time zone using location data (provided location settings are switched on).

To change the time zone:

1. Click **Start** () to display the Start menu.
2. Click **Settings** () to open the Settings app.
3. Click **Time & Language**.
4. Click **Date & Time**.
5. Click the **Time Zone** list and then click your time zone.

After you select a time zone, Windows will adjust the time as appropriate.

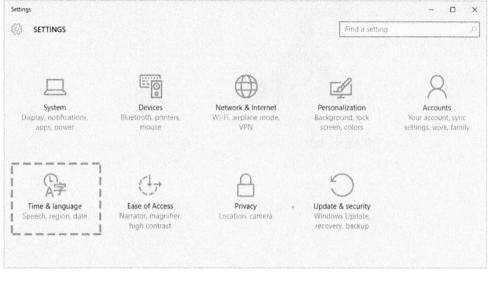

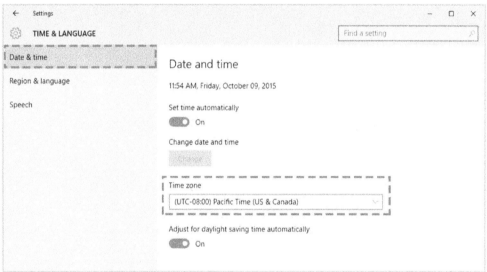

If you are in a location where daylight saving time doesn't apply, you typically will need to enable or disable daylight saving time manually when you are using a desktop, laptop or tablet PC. Other times, such as when you have a smart phone or small tablet running a mobile edition of Windows 10, the device may be able to configure the daylight saving time appropriately using location data (provided location settings are on).

To switch daylight saving time on or off:

1. Click **Start** (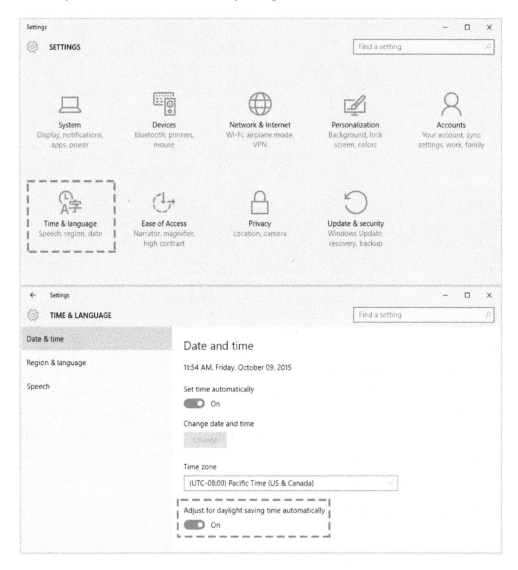) to display the Start menu.

2. Click **Settings** ( ) to open the Settings app.

3. Click **Time & Language**.

4. Click **Date & Time**.

5. Click **Adjust For Daylight Saving Time Automatically** to **On** to allow the device to adjust the time. Click the switch to **Off** to prevent the device from adjusting the time.

Configuring Cortana

Cortana is a voice-activated digital assistant. If your Windows device has a built-in microphone or you've connected one to your device, you can use Cortana to help you keep up with day-to-day tasks and activities. For example, you can ask Cortana about appointments or request that you get a reminder at a specific time or location. Once configured, you can also use Cortana to perform searches using your voice.

To activate Cortana:

1. Start the Cortana setup process by clicking in the Search box. If the Search box isn't displayed on the taskbar, click **Start** and then click in the Search box.
2. If Cortana setup doesn't start, click the Cortana

   button ().
3. When Cortana starts, click **Next** to continue.

4. Click **I Agree** to accept the Cortana user agreement.
5. When prompted, type your name or whatever you'd like to be Cortana to call you.
6. Click **Next**.
7. Click **Got it**.

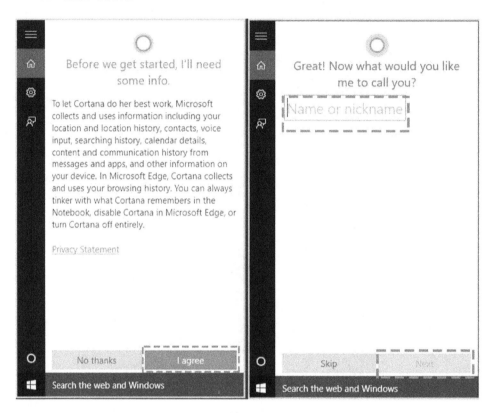

You'll now be able to use Cortana to search your device and get assistance.

Using Cortana

You can use Cortana in several different ways. By default, you must click

the **Talk** () button before you can ask about anything.

When you speak to Cortana, you simply use your natural voice and language. Here are some examples for using Cortana as your assistant:

- "Add 10 AM meeting with John to my calendar for Monday."
- "Set an alarm for 6:00 AM."
- "Play my music."
- "What song is playing?"
- "What's the Mariner's score?"
- "How far to Seattle, Washington?"
- "What's traffic like today?"
- "When does Olive Garden open?"

Here are some examples for using Cortana for searches:

- "Show my recent emails."
- "Find my recent Word documents."
- "Show documents created last week."
- "Show me today's headlines."

If you don't want to have to click the Talk button each time, you can configure your device so that Cortana is always on and responds to "Hey Cortana." Although this setting uses more battery and means your device is always listening, it is handy when you are working with Cortana frequently or don't have your hands free, such as when you are driving.

To configure your device to always listen:

1. Click the **Talk** () button. If the Search box isn't displayed on the taskbar, click **Start** and then click the Talk button.

2. Click the **Notebook** () button.

3. Click the **Settings** () button.

4. Click the **Let Cortana Respond...** switch to **On**.

5. By default, Cortana responds when anyone says "Hey Cortana." If you want Cortana to respond only when you speak, click **Learn My Voice**, then follow the prompts.

If you no longer want Cortana to be always enabled, repeat this procedure but set the **Let Cortana Respond...** switch to **Off**.

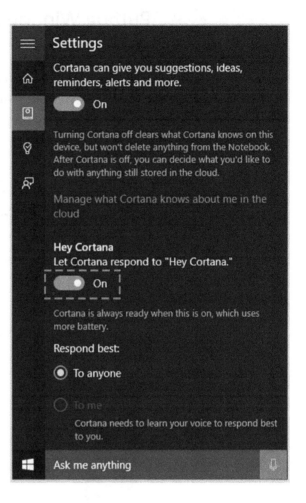

Putting Windows to Sleep

No, Windows isn't Old Yeller and you don't have to put it down (unless you really want to). That said, you can make your device more energy efficient by putting Windows into sleep mode when you aren't using your device.

In sleep mode, Windows 10 saves the state of your desktop and running apps and then enters a low-power mode to save energy—and your battery if your device is running on battery power. When you resume Windows from sleep mode, after you sign in (if required), Windows restores the state of your desktop and running apps so you can quickly and efficiently get back to work.

> **TIP**: Newer devices support Hyperboot and Instant Go. Hyperboot enables superfast startup of the operating system whenever you start or restart. Instant Go enables superfast resume whenever you wake the device from sleep.

To put Windows to sleep:

1. Click **Start** ( ) to display the Start menu.
2. Click **Power** ( ) to display the Power options.
3. Click **Sleep**.

To wake a desktop or laptop from sleep mode, press the device's power button. With tablets and small devices, such as a smart phone, wake the device from sleep mode by pressing the Home button (located on the front of the device).

You can also configure your device to automatically go to sleep after it has been idle for a specified amount of time. To configure your device to go to sleep automatically:

1. Click **Start** (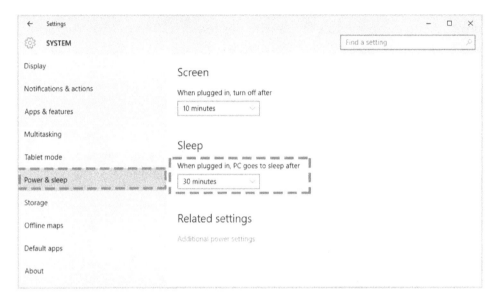) to display the Start menu.

2. Click **Settings** ( ) to open the Settings app.

3. Click **System**, then click **Power & Sleep**.

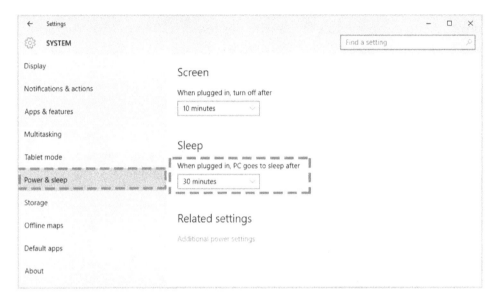

4. Under **Sleep**, use the **When Plugged In, Turn Off After** list to specify the number of minutes of idle time before Windows goes to sleep when running on A/C power.

5. If available, use the **On Battery, Turn Off After** list under the **Sleep** heading to specify the number of minutes of idle time before Windows goes to sleep when running on battery power.

Restarting or Shutting Down Windows

Sleep and resume works wonderfully—until it doesn't. That's because Windows may start to slow down over time as you stop and start the operating system. Windows may also start acting funny (meaning erratic) over time. This can occur because resources don't get freed up properly or processes continue to run when they shouldn't. Don't worry there's a quick fix.

To get Windows running efficiently again, do a restart. A restart shuts the device down and then immediately starts it up again.

> **TIP**: I recommend restarting Windows periodically to keep your device running at its peak performance. How often? Minimally, once a month, so when you look at the calendar and it's the first of the month, give your device a restart!

To restart Windows:

1. Click **Start** ( ) to display the Start menu.

2. Click **Power** ( ) to display the Power options.
3. Click **Restart**.

At times, you also may want to completely power down your device. To do this, you shut down Windows. Shutting down ensures Windows doesn't use any additional power (which saves your battery if your device isn't plugged in to AC power).

> **TIP**: The shutdown state is also the only time you should open the cover on your device, unplug your device or remove the battery in your device.

To shut down Windows:

1. Click **Start** ( ) to display the Start menu.

2. Click **Power** ( ) to display the Power options.

3. Click **Shut Down**.

Connecting to the World

If your device has built-in wireless networking, you can connect to a wireless access point to access wireless networks. Connecting to a network allows you to access any resources hosted on the network. If the wireless access point also is connected to the Internet, then connecting to the wireless network allows your device to access the Internet.

There are two general types of wireless networks:

- Open
- Secured

Open networks, often listed as Guest networks when you visit a coffee shop or other retailer, typically don't require you to use a security key or password. They do, however, generally require you to accept service terms and sign in.

In contrast, secured networks require you to have a security key or password to access the network. They may also require you to accept service terms and sign in.

To connect to an open wireless network:

1. Click **Network** () to display the Network sidebar.
2. Click the network that you want to connect to.
3. To have Windows connect automatically in the future, click **Connect Automatically**. The related checkbox will then have a checkmark.
4. Click **Connect**.
5. Wait a few seconds. If sign-in is required, Windows should prompt you. Click **Yes**.
6. Windows opens a browser window. If prompted, accept the terms of service, and then click the option provided for connecting to the network. Otherwise, simply click the option provided for connecting.

> **TIP**: Sometimes the option for accepting the terms of service is a tiny checkbox that's hardly visible. Here, do your best to tap or click in the checkbox. When selected, the box will have a checkmark inside it.

To connect to a secured wireless network or an open network with a password:

1. Click **Network** () to display the Network sidebar.
2. Click the network that you want to connect to.
3. To have Windows connect automatically in the future, click **Connect Automatically**. The related checkbox will then have a checkmark.
4. Click **Connect**.
5. Enter the security key or password when prompted. If needed, click and hold the reveal button () to temporarily display the characters you entered.
6. Click **Next**.

Windows may prompt you to confirm whether it can locate other computers or devices on the network. If you are on your home network, click **Yes**. Otherwise, click **No**.

If additional sign-in is required or acceptance of service terms is required, Windows may also prompt you. Click **Yes**. If prompted, accept the terms of service, and then click the option provided for connecting or agreeing. Otherwise, simply click the option provided for connecting or agreeing.

> **TIP**: Sometimes when sign in is required, Windows won't open a browser window with the additional options needed for sign in. If this happens, click **Microsoft Edge** () on the taskbar and then enter a web address in the browser window or simply try to browse to a web address, such as www.yahoo.com. This should force Windows to open the sign-in page.

If you don't want Windows to be connected to a network any more, you can disconnect from the network:

1. Click **Network** () to display the Network sidebar.
2. Click the network to which you are connected.
3. Click **Disconnect** to disconnect from the wireless network.

Checking & Conserving Your Battery

When you are working with a laptop, tablet or other mobile device, you'll often want to determine the remaining battery power. You may also want to confirm whether your device is charging when you plug it in to AC power.

The power icon on the taskbar acts as an indicator that provides a representation of the current power level of your battery and charging status:

Indicates the battery has about a 35% charge

Indicates the battery has about a 65% charge

Indicates the battery is fully charged (or nearly so).

Indicates your device is plugged in and charging.

> **TIP:** When your device is plugged in and charging, the relative power indicator bar is much more precise. In the example show above, the battery is 90% or more charged.

To determine the exact battery level:

1. Click **Power** ().
2. The current battery level and status is displayed.

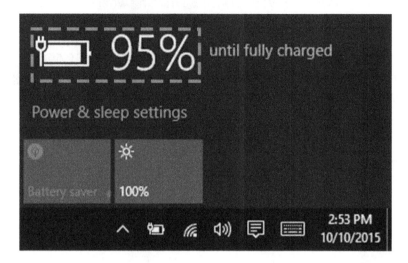

Windows includes a battery-saving mode that is designed to increase your device's battery life by dimming the screen, restricting the maximum processor speed and making other power-saving adjustments.

You can easily determine whether your device is using battery-saving mode by the power icon on the taskbar. When this mode is enabled, the icon has a power-saving symbol:

To manage battery-saving mode:

1. Click **Power** ( ).
2. To enable battery-saving mode, click **Battery Saver** to **On** (highlighted).
3. To enable battery-saving mode, click **Battery Saver** to **Off** (dimmed).

Day 4

Connecting Your Account

Day 4.
Connecting Your Account

Lesson Notes: Windows has several different types of user accounts. In Day 4, you'll learn how to make your user account a connected one and how to configure a connected account.

Windows has always supported several different types of user accounts. Windows 10 introduces a new option for user accounts that allows you to connect your user account to a Microsoft account. Your user account then becomes a connected account that:

- Has full access to many previously inaccessible Windows features, including OneDrive for storing your documents and photos online
- Can download universal apps from the Windows Store and use the apps on any device to which you can log in
- Can use unified settings to customize certain aspects of the operating system and have those same settings whenever you log in to your account on any device.

Ready to learn how to use connected accounts?

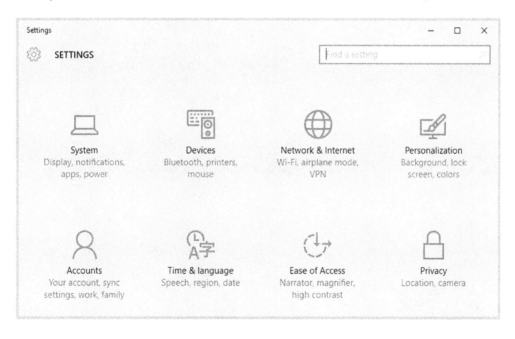

Do I Have a Connected Account...

Whether you have a connected account depends on how you set up your Windows 10 device. If you upgraded your device to Windows 10 from an earlier version of Windows, you probably have a standard user account. If you purchased a device with Windows 10 already installed, you probably have a connected account.

To determine if you have a connected account:

1. Click **Start** (   ) to display the Start menu.

2. Click **Settings** (   ) to open the Settings app.
3. Click **Accounts** to display the Accounts window.

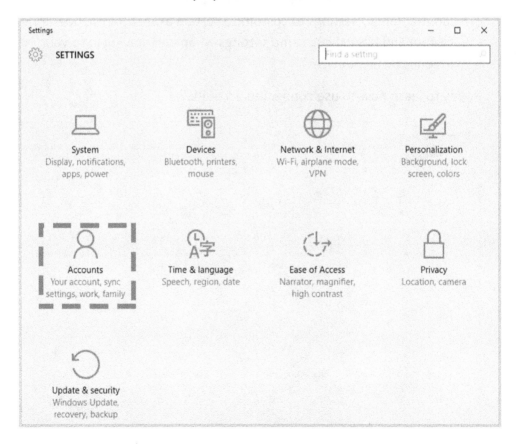

4. If you have a local account, Local Account is listed under your user name and you have an option to **Sign In With A Microsoft Account Instead**.

TIP: You also can determine whether you have a connected account by looking at your user name. If your user name looks like an email address, such as bob.roberts.training@gmail.com, then you have a connected account. Otherwise, you have a standard user account.

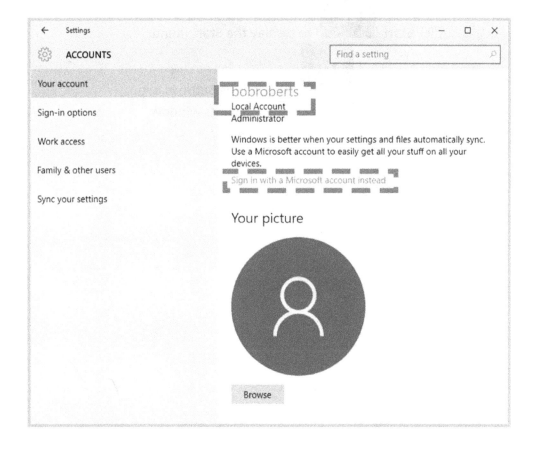

Switching to a Microsoft Account

If your user account isn't connected to a Microsoft account, you can connect to a Microsoft account at any time to get the advantages of having a connected account.

To switch to a Microsoft account:

1. Click **Start** (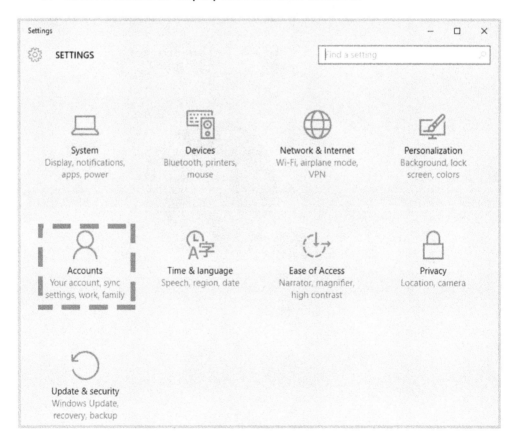) to display the Start menu.

2. Click **Settings** ( ) to open the Settings app.
3. Click **Accounts** to display the Accounts window.

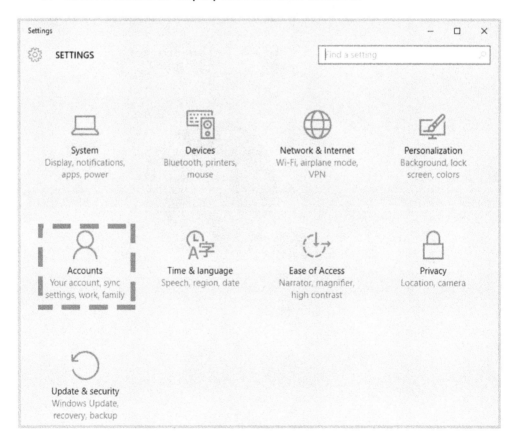

4. Click **Sign In With A Microsoft Account Instead** to display the
    Make It Yours window.

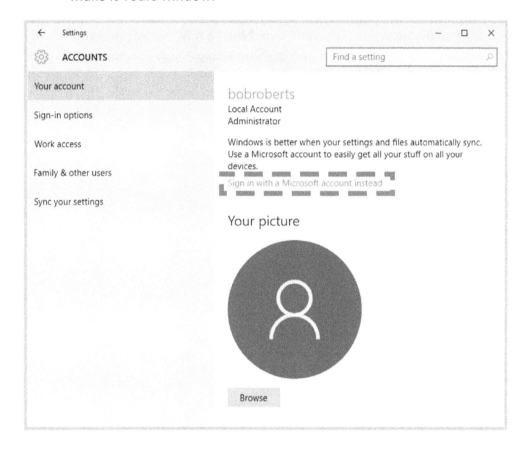

When you are working with the Make It Yours window, you have two
options:

*   If you have an existing Microsoft account, you can connect it to
    your user account as discussed in **Connecting Your Existing
    Account**.
*   Otherwise, you need to create a new Microsoft account and
    connect it to your user account as discussed in **Configuring a New
    Account**.

Connecting Your Existing Account

After following Steps 1-4 under **Switching To A Microsoft Account**, connect your existing Microsoft account to your user account by following these steps:

1. Type the email address associated with the Microsoft account, such as bob.roberts.training@gmail.com.
2. Type the password for the Microsoft account.
3. Click **Sign In**.

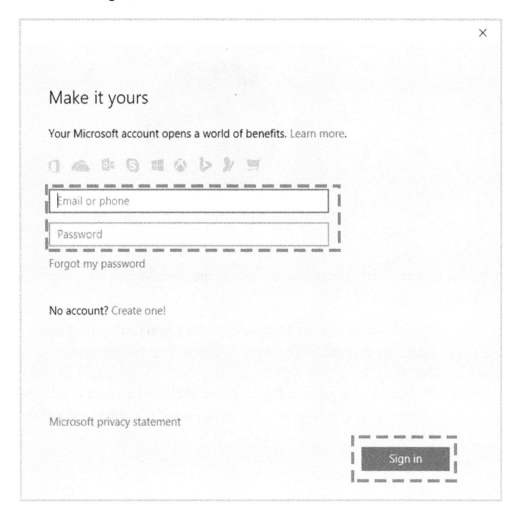

4. Choose an option when Windows asks how you want to receive your security code to verify your account.
5. Click **Next**.
6. Type the password for your local user account. If your user account doesn't have a password, leave the box blank.

7. Click **Next**.
8. Windows asks if you want to use a PIN with your account. For now, click **Skip This Step**. Don't worry, you can create a PIN later.

Windows connects the Microsoft account to your user account. The next time you start Windows, you will need to use your Microsoft account email address and the password for your Microsoft account to sign in.

TIP: Don't forget you still need to verify your identity on your Windows device. See **Verifying Your Account**.

Configuring a New Account

After following Steps 1-4 under **Switching To A Microsoft Account**, connect a new Microsoft account to your user account by following these steps:

1. Click **Create One** in the Make It Yours window.

2. Type your first and last name.
3. Specify the email address you want to use. If you have an email account that you want to use, enter this email address and proceed to the next step. Otherwise, click **Get A New Email**

Address. Next, type the user name you want to use with Outlook. Your new email address will be *username*@outlook.com.

4. Type the password you want to use with your Microsoft account.
5. Select your country.
6. Specify your date of birth.
7. Click **Next**.

You next need to provide additional security information so if you ever forget your password Microsoft can send you text message to help you reset your password. If you don't have a mobile phone, you can provide Microsoft with an alternative email address instead and then this email address will be used verifying your identity if you ever forget your password.

1. If you want to associate a mobile phone number with your account. Select your phone number's country code and then type your mobile phone number. Click **Next**.
2. If you want to associate an alternative email address with your account instead of a mobile phone number, click **Add An Alternate Email Instead**. Type the alternate email address and then click **Next**.
3. Choose an option when Windows asks how you want to receive your security code to verify your account and then click **Next**.
4. Type the password for your local user account. If your account doesn't have a password, leave the box blank.
5. Click **Next**.
6. Windows asks if you want to use a PIN with your account. For now, click **Skip This Step**. Don't worry, you can create a PIN later.
7. That's it, you're done!

Windows connects the Microsoft account to your user account. The next time you start Windows, you will need to use your Microsoft account email address and the password for your Microsoft account to sign in.

> **TIP**: Don't forget you still need to verify your identity on your Windows device. See **Verifying Your Account**.

Verifying Your Account

If you used an existing email address when switching to a Microsoft account, you must verify the account to confirm your identity on the device. Verifying your identity means entering the confirmation code sent to the mobile phone number or alternate email address associated with your account.

To verify your account:

1. Click **Start** ( ) to display the Start menu.

2. Click **Settings** ( ) to open the Settings app.
3. Click **Accounts** to display the Accounts window.

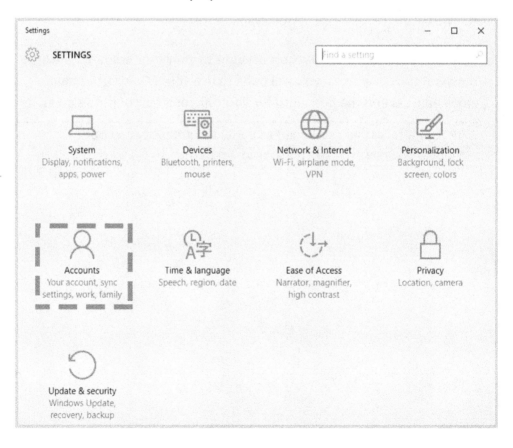

4. Click **Your Account** and then click **Verify.**

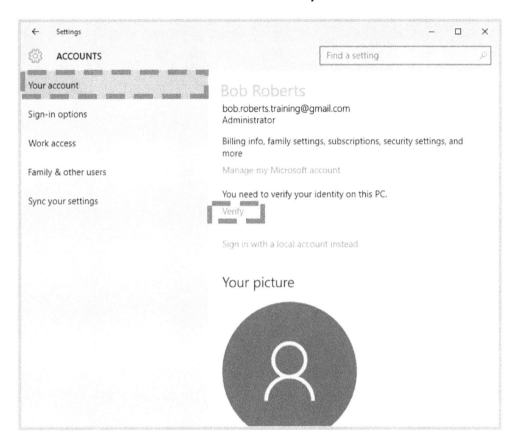

5. Do one of the following:

A. If you already have a code from when you set up your account, click **I Have a Code** and then skip Steps 6, 7 and 8.

B. If you don't have a code or it's been a long time since you were provided the code, select an option under **How Would You Like To Get This Code**.

6. If you want to get the code via text, type the last 4 digits of the mobile phone number.

7. If you want to get the code via email, type the email address.

8. Click **Next**. The code is sent to you via text or email. It may take up to 5 minutes. Read the email or text when you receive it and note the code.

9. Type the code and then click **Next**.

(A) Help us protect your info

When accessing sensitive info from your account or device, or if we detect suspicious account activity, we'll ask for a security code to verify your identity. (If you sign in frequently on this device, we won't ask you to verify after this.)

How would you like to get this code?

Text (***) ***-**05

To verify that this is your phone number, enter the last 4 digits including 05, and then click "Next" to receive your code.

Last 4 digits

I have a code

Next   Back

(B) Help us protect your info

When accessing sensitive info from your account or device, or if we detect suspicious account activity, we'll ask for a security code to verify your identity. (If you sign in frequently on this device, we won't ask you to verify after this.)

How would you like to get this code?

Text (***) ***-**05

To verify that this is your phone number, enter the last 4 digits including 05, and then click "Next" to receive your code.

Last 4 digits

I have a code

Next   Back

That's it, your account is verified.

> **TIP**: If for some reason verification doesn't work, simply repeat this procedure and try using a different verification option.

Syncing Your Settings

If you have more than one device running Windows 10, you can use the same Microsoft account on each device and get the connected benefits I talked about earlier, including access to your universal apps and unified settings. This gives you a consistent working environment across your devices and consistent access to your data.

To sync data between your devices:

1. Click **Start** (   ) to display the Start menu.

2. Click **Settings** (   ) to open the Settings app.
3. Click **Accounts** to display the Accounts window.

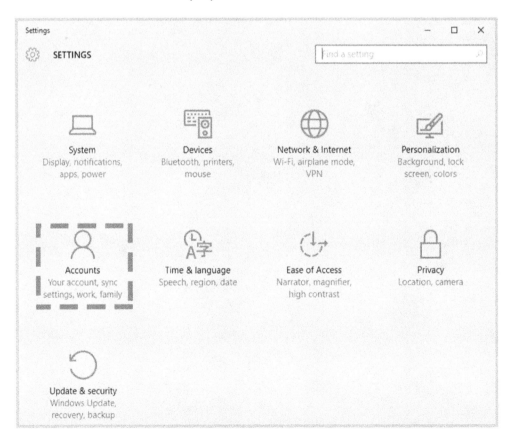

4. Click **Sync Your Settings**.
5. Click the **Sync Settings** switch to **On**.

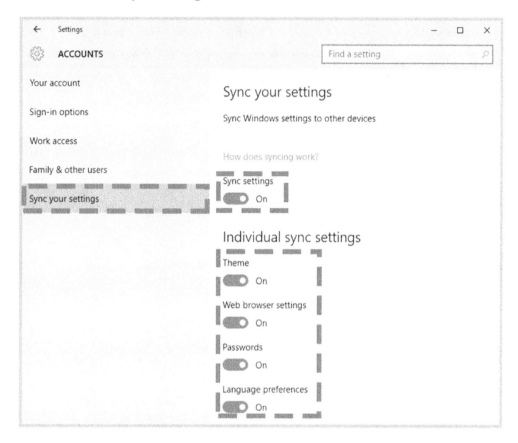

6. Under Individual Sync Settings, all switches are On by default. Click the switch to **Off** for any setting that you do not want to sync.

TIP: If you toggle sync switches on or off, those changes are applied the next time Windows syncs.

Enabling Device Location

Location settings are an important part of staying connected and connecting to the world whenever you use your Windows device. Many Windows features and apps rely on location settings being enabled and won't function properly if these settings are turned off.

Windows manages location settings on a per device and per account basis. Location must be enabled both for the device and your account in order for Windows to identify the location of your device.

To view and modify location settings:

1. Click **Start** (   ) to display the Start menu.

2. Click **Settings** (   ) to open the Settings app.
3. Click **Privacy** to display the Privacy window.

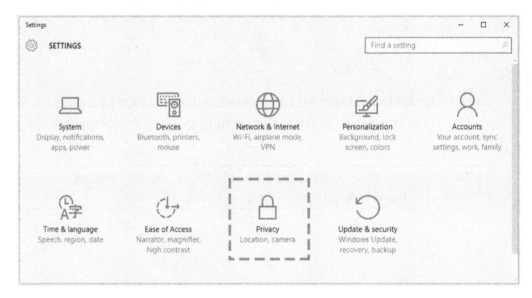

4. Click **Location** to display the Location page.
5. If location settings for the device are disabled, the Location page states **Location for this device is off**. To enable location for the

device, click **Change**, then click the **Location For This Device** switch to **On**.

6. If location settings for your account are disabled, the Location switch is **Off** (and the setting is dimmed and barely readable). To enable location for your account, click the **Location** switch to **On**.

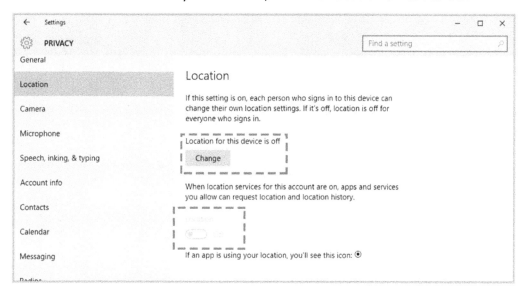

Day 5

Getting and Using Apps

Day 5.
Getting and Using Apps

Lesson Notes: In Day 5, you learn basic techniques for working with apps.

Before we get started, let's take a moment to discuss what exactly a universal app is and how it's different from traditional software. The term universal app is a general usage for all the various types of programs that you can download from the Windows Store, including business and education software, productivity programs and security utilities. Universal apps can be downloaded and used on any Windows 10 device to which you log in with your Microsoft account.

Although Microsoft puts games in a separate area of the store from general apps, the games you download from the store are also apps. In the store, apps are available as either free or paid downloads. Although free downloads typically also offer in-app purchases, you aren't obligated to purchase anything extra.

Windows 10 also supports other types of programs, including traditional software installed from media or downloaded from the Internet outside of the Windows Store.

- If you purchased software from a retail store and installation media, such as a DVD-ROM or USB flash drive, was included, you install the software using the installation media.
- If you downloaded software from the Internet, double-click the file you downloaded to start the installation process and then follow the installation instructions.

> **TIP**: Keep in mind traditional software doesn't have the benefits of universal apps. When you install traditional software, you generally can only use the software on the device on which it is installed. If you want to use the software on other devices you log into (and licensing allows), you must install the software before it is available for use.

Getting Apps, Games & More

You get apps from the Windows Store. To access the store, you must have an Internet connection as discussed under **Connecting to the World** in Day 3. Additionally, as you need a Microsoft account to install apps, see **Switching to a Microsoft Account** in Day 4 if you don't have one.

To install an app from the Windows Store:

1. Click **Store** ( ) on the taskbar to access the Windows Store.

TIP: If the store icon isn't available on the taskbar, click **Start** and then click **Store** on the Start menu.

---

2. The Windows Store has options for browsing and searching to find apps, including:

A. Tabs for browsing the store.
B. Search box for finding apps.
C. Icons for apps that are available.

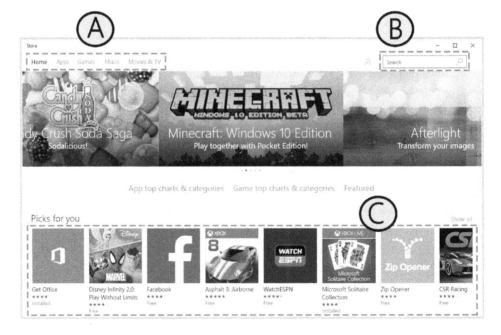

3. Use the tabs or the Search box to find an app to install.
4. Click the app to display the related product page.
5. Download and buy options are provided:

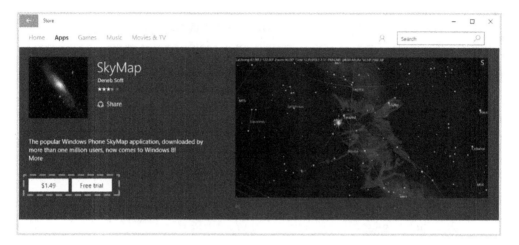

- If the app is free, click **Get** or **Free**.
- If the app isn't free, there's a price button instead and sometimes an option for a free trial. Click the price button to buy, type your Microsoft account password and then click OK.

6. Windows downloads and installs the app.

> **TIP**: The Windows Store also has music, movies and television shows. You purchase music, movies and television shows in the store in the same way you purchase apps and games.

Starting Apps & Games

The way you use and work with Windows 10 is all about the apps installed. To check the weather, you use the Weather app. You check current events using the News app and create appointment reminders using the Calendar app. To browse the web, you use the Microsoft Edge app. All of these apps and more are available via the Start Menu and the All Apps list.

To start an app using the Start Menu:

1. Click **Start** ( ) to display the Start menu.
2. Click the icon for the app you want to open.

3. Close the app when you are finished by clicking **Close** ( ).

To start an app using the All Apps list:

1. Click **Start** () to display the Start menu.

2. Click **All Apps** ( ) to display the All Apps sidebar.
3. The All Apps list is organized alphabetically. Scroll until you see the app you want to run.
4. Click the icon for the app you want to open.
5. Close the app when you are finished by clicking **Close** (☒).

Some apps are pinned to the taskbar. If so, you can start the app simply by clicking the icon on the taskbar.

> **TIP**: Want to pin an app to the taskbar so you can start it quickly? See **Pinning Apps** in Day 5.

Working with App Menus

Universal apps can have either a traditional or modern interface. The traditional interface, with a ribbon across the top, tabs and menus, is probably something you've seen before. Most Windows accessories and administrative tools have this interface, as these accessories and tools have been a part of Windows for many years and are used in many earlier releases of Windows. In contrast, the modern interface is something you see in apps designed specifically for Windows 8 and later.

Apps with the modern interface typically don't have a ribbon across the top and instead have an app menu that runs down the left side of the window. This menu gives you access to features, options and settings. By default, the app menu shows only icons for available options, but you can open the menu to display the names of each option.

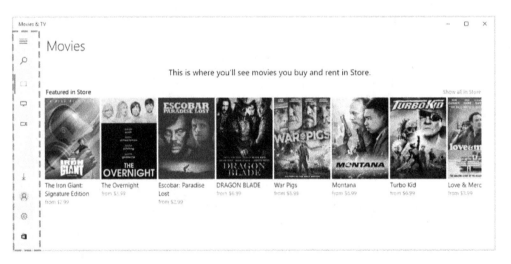

To access an app's options:

1. Open the app that you want to work with.

2. Click **Menu** (☰) to expand the menu and show the available options.

3. Click the option you want to use.

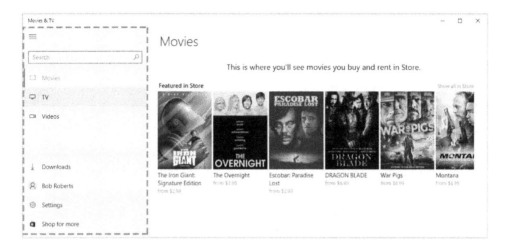

When you select an option, the app automatically hides the menu. If you want to hide the menu without selecting an option, simply click **Menu** again.

Many apps have additional settings that aren't available on the menu. To access these settings:

1. Click **Menu** ( ) to expand the menu and show the available options.

2. Click **Settings** ( ).
3. Use the options provided to configure app settings.

Switching Between Apps

Windows is a multitasking operating system that allows you to run multiple apps at once without having to close the app you are using before starting another one. As an example, during the course of the day, you may use a word processor, email app, web browser and calendar app. If so, you don't need to close the word processor before you can open the email app and you don't need to close the word processor or email app to open the web browser or the calendar app. All of these apps can run at the same time.

When you run multiple apps at once, you need to know how to switch from one app to another. One way to do this is to use the taskbar. You can also use a special view called Task view.

To switch between apps using the taskbar:

1. Move the mouse pointer over the taskbar button of the program you want to switch to. Windows displays a thumbnail version of the app window.
2. Click the app's taskbar button to bring the app window to the front so you can work with it.

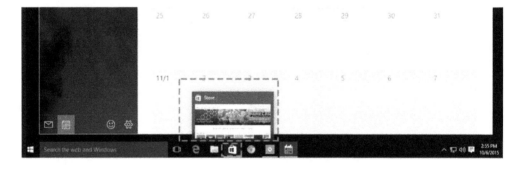

To switch between apps using Task view:

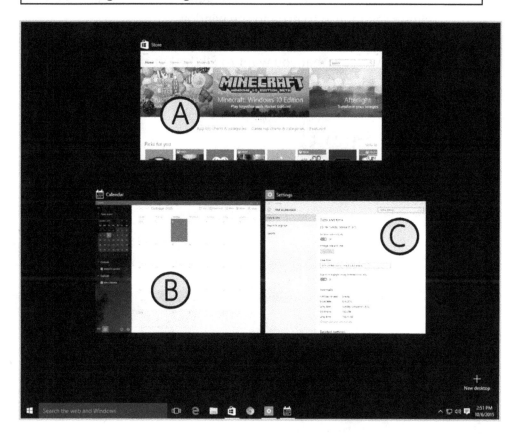

1. Click the **Task View** ( ) button on the taskbar. In Task View, Windows displays a preview of the apps running on the currently selected desktop.
2. Click the thumbnail of the app that you want to bring to the front so you can work with it.

TIP: You also can switch to another app simply by clicking in the app window. When an app is in the front of all other apps, the app is said to be running in the foreground.

Arranging Apps

Rather than switching back and forth between windows, you'll sometimes want to arrange windows on the desktop so that they are side by side. Windows 10 allows you to do this using a feature called snap.

The most basic way to use snap is to arrange two windows so that they are side by side with one filling the right half of the screen and the other filling the left half of the screen:

1. Drag the title bar of the first window to the right side of the screen until an outline of the expanded window appears, then release the mouse to expand the window.
2. The Task View is displayed showing other open windows.
3. Click the window that you want to fill the left side of the screen.

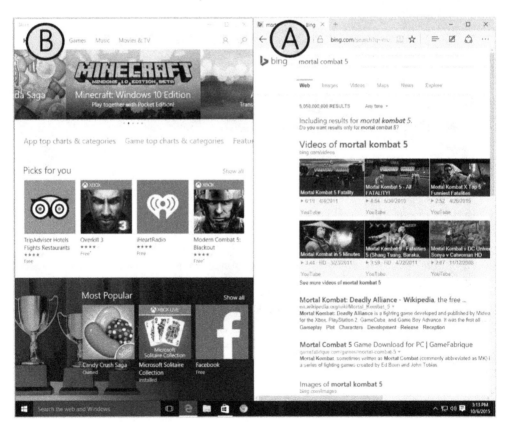

Use the Windows logo ( ) key and arrow keys to arrange two windows side by side as well:

1. Press the Windows logo ( ) key and the Right Arrow key to snap a window to the right.
2. When you release the pressed keys, the Task view is displayed showing other open windows.
3. Click the window that you want to fill the left side of the screen.

In addition to snapping two windows side by side, you can snap a window to a quarter of the screen by dragging a window to any corner. You also can use the Windows logo ( ) key to snap a window to a quarter of the screen:

1. Press the Windows logo ( ) key and the Left or Right Arrow key to snap a window to the left or right.
2. Press the Windows logo ( ) key and the Up or Down Arrow key to snap the window to the upper or lower corner.

Pinning Apps

Windows 10 provides several ways to make it easier for you to start and use favorite apps. The first technique involves pinning an app shortcut to the taskbar. You also can pin apps to the Start Menu. With either option, you must first find the app you can to work with on the All Apps list.

To pin an app to the taskbar:

1. Click **Start** ( ).

2. Click **All Apps** ( ).
3. Scroll until you see the app.
4. Right-click the icon for the app and then select **Pin To Taskbar**.

To pin an app to Start:

1. Click **Start** (![Start icon]) to display the Start menu.

2. Click **All Apps** (![All Apps icon]) to display the All Apps sidebar.
3. Scroll until you see the app you want to run.
4. Right-click the icon for the app you want to pin and then select **Pin To Start**.

When you pin an app to Start, the app is represented by a tile, which you can click to start the app. As discussed previously, tiles replace the traditional program icons used in Windows 7 and earlier releases of Windows.

You can move tiles around the Start menu simply by clicking and dragging a tile to a new location. You can resize apps to make them smaller or larger.

To resize an app:

1. Click **Start** () to display the Start menu.
2. Right-click the app tile on Start.
3. Click **Resize**.
4. Click the tile size to use.

Unpin from Start	
Resize >	Small
Turn live tile off	✓ Medium
Pin to taskbar	Wide

Adding Apps to the Lock Screen

The Lock screen is displayed whenever you wake or start your device. It's also displayed when you lock your device.

By default, the Lock screen displays the current time and date. The Lock screen can also show notifications and provide status updates for certain system apps, including:

- Alarms & Clock
- Calendar
- Mail
- People
- Store
- Weather
- Xbox

Typically, the only apps added to the Lock screen by default are Mail and Calendar. To determine which apps, if any, have been added to the lock screen:

1. Click **Start** (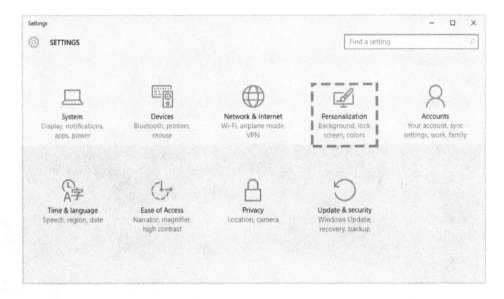) to display the Start menu.

2. Click **Settings** ( ) to open the Settings app.
3. Click **Personalization** to display the Personalization page.

Settings				– □ ✕
⚙ SETTINGS			Find a setting	🔍

System	Devices	Network & Internet	Personalization	Accounts
Display, notifications, apps, power	Bluetooth, printers, mouse	Wi-Fi, airplane mode, VPN	Background, lock screen, colors	Your account, sync settings, work, family

Time & language	Ease of Access	Privacy	Update & security	
Speech, region, date	Narrator, magnifier, high contrast	Location, camera	Windows Update, recovery, backup	

4. Click **Lock Screen**.

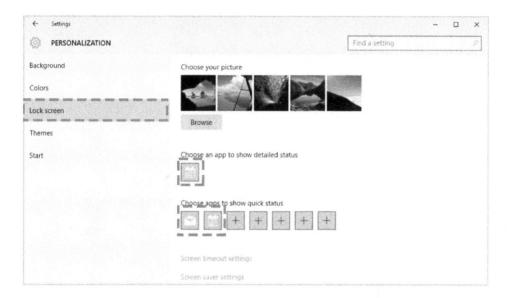

5. Note which apps are selected for detailed status and quick status updates:

- Only one app can display detailed status updates and notifications on the Lock screen. If a detailed status app is currently selected, it's icon is displayed under **Choose Apps To Show Detailed Status**. If no detailed status app is selected, you'll see the **Add** ( ) option instead.

- Up to seven apps app can display quick status updates and notifications on the Lock screen. If quick status apps are currently selected, the related icons are displayed under **Choose Apps To Show Quick Status**. If no quick status app is selected for one of the seven slots, you'll see the **Add** ( ) option instead.

To add an app to the lock screen:

1. Click **Start** (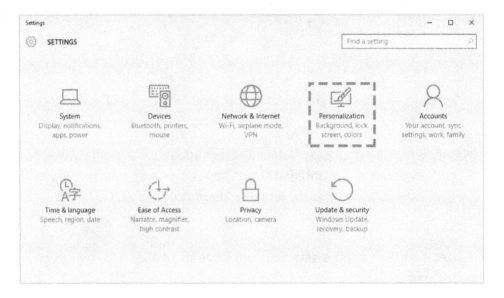) to display the Start menu.

2. Click **Settings** ( ) to open the Settings app.

3. Click **Personalization** to display the Personalization page.

4. Click **Lock Screen**.

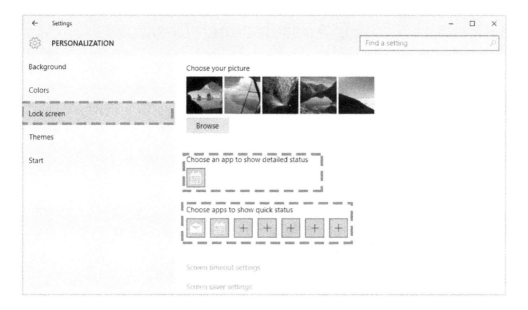

5. To select the detailed status app, click the box under **Choose An App To Show Detailed Status** and then click the App to use.

6. To select a quick status app, click a box under **Choose Apps To Show Quick Status** and then click the App to use.

TIP: There are seven slots for quick status apps. To replace an existing app, click its icon and then select a different app. To add a quick status

app without replacing an existing app, use the **Add** (⊞) option instead and fill a different slot.

Moving Apps Between Desktops

Anytime you are working with multiple desktops, you may find that you want to move apps from one desktop to another. You use the Task view to do this.

To move apps between desktops:

1. Click the **Task View** (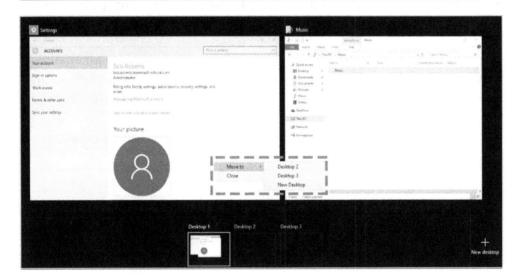) button on the taskbar.
2. Right-click the app you want to move.
3. Click **Move To**.
4. Click the desktop to which you want to move the app.

> **TIP**: You also can move the app to a new desktop. To do this, click **Move To** and then select **New Desktop**.

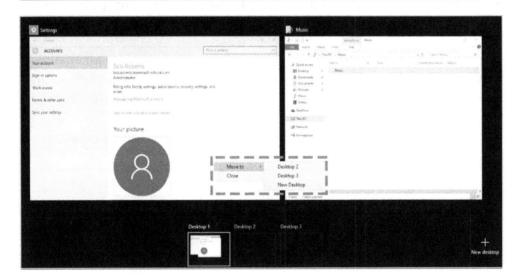

Day 6

More Tips & Tricks for Apps

Day 6.
More Tips & Tricks for Apps

Lesson Notes: In Day 6, you learn more tips and tricks for working with apps.

Most of the time when you are using Windows you are working with apps, so it's a good idea to learn about some of the key apps and get more tips and tricks for working with apps. For this reason, today's lessons continue the apps discussion started in the previous day and provides information about keeping apps up to date and removing apps you no longer want on your device.

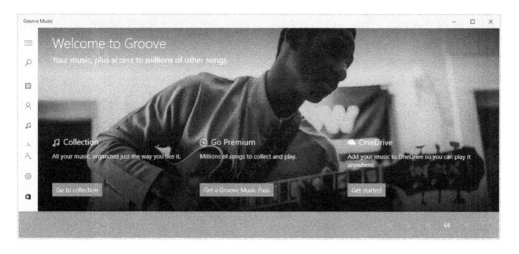

Updating Apps Manually

A unified update process is another benefit of universal apps. Instead of having to update each of your apps separately as you need to with traditional software, universal apps have centralized updates through the Windows Store. As apps and games are updated periodically by their developers to add features, enhance existing features, and fix issues, the updates are made available and you can download and install the updates.

To update apps:

1. Click **Store** (![Store icon]) on the taskbar to access the Windows Store.

> **TIP**: If the store icon isn't available on the taskbar, click **Start** and then click **Store** on the Start menu.

2. In the upper-right corner of the Store window, you have options for Downloads and Settings.

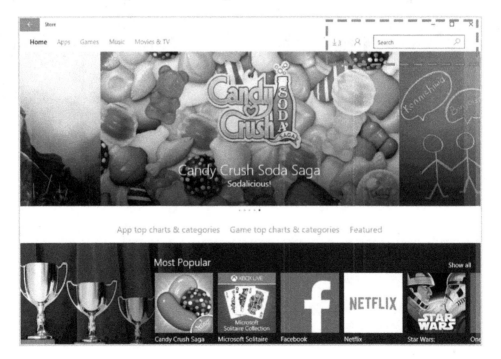

A. If downloads and updates are queued and ready, you'll see the number available. Click **Downloads** () here to display the Downloads And Updates page.

B. If there aren't any downloads or updates waiting, it doesn't mean there aren't any available. Click **Account** ( ) and then click **Downloads And Updates**.

3. The Downloads And Updates page shows any queued downloads and updates. To ensure you are viewing all available downloads and updates, click **Check For Updates**.

4. To update all the apps at once, click **Update All**.

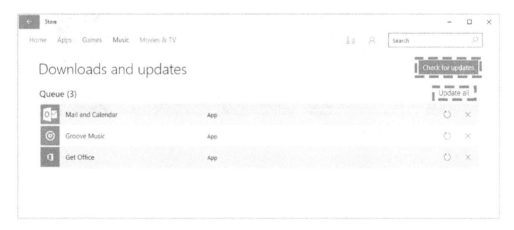

Updating Apps Automatically

Instead of updating apps manually, you can configure Windows to automatically download and install updates for apps. To update apps automatically:

1. Click **Store** ( ) on the taskbar to access the Windows Store.

TIP: If the store icon isn't available on the taskbar, click **Start** and then click **Store** on the Start menu.

2. In the upper-right corner of the Store window, you have options for Downloads and Settings.

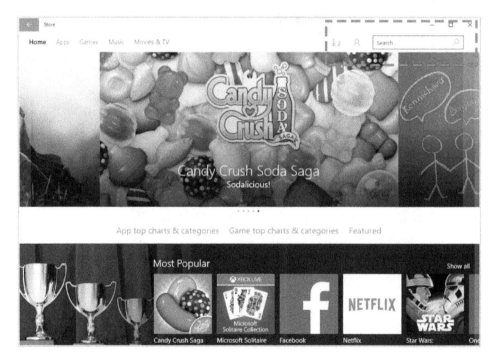

3. Click **Account** () in the upper-right corner of the Store window and then click **Settings**.

4. Click the **Update Apps Automatically** switch to **On**.

TIP: Once configured, this automatic update process is then performed as part of the housekeeping tasks Windows performs daily. However, if your device doesn't have an Internet connection or is shut down at the scheduled time the automatic check is to be performed, Windows won't be able to update apps automatically.

TIP: With some apps, including those that are available by default, the automatic update process doesn't work properly and the only way to find out about updates is to use the manual process discussed in the previous section.

Allowing Apps to Use Location Data

Location data is required for apps to identify where your device is located and then use this information to provide you with customized information. Some examples:

- The Weather app uses your location to provide local weather by default.
- Windows Maps uses your location to find your exact location and use this as the starting point whenever you work with the app.
- Windows and Cortana use your location anytime you use search features, such as restaurants near me.

Rather than allowing all apps to access location data automatically, Windows allows you to control which apps have access to location information. This approach is meant to help protect your privacy.

To specify which apps can use location information:

1. Click **Start** () to display the Start menu.

2. Click **Settings** () to open the Settings app.
3. Click **Privacy** to display the Privacy window.

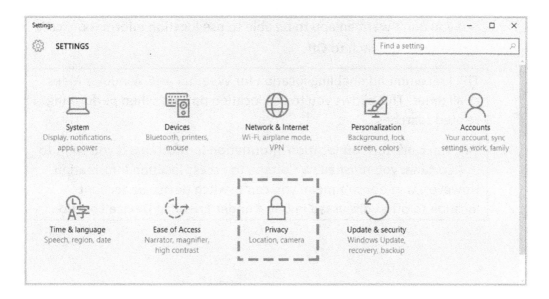

4. Click **Location** to display the Location page.

Each installed app that can use location information is listed under the **Choose Apps That Can Use Your Location** heading.

- If you want an app to be able to use location information, click the related switch to **On**.

- If you don't want an app to be able to use location information, click the related switch to **Off**.

> **TIP**: I recommend enabling location for Weather and Windows Maps at all times. This allows you to use location options when performing related searches.
>
> **TIP**: You can't turn off location information for Cortana. If you want to use Cortana, you must allow Cortana to access location information. However, that doesn't mean you can't switch device or account location to off as discussed in Day 4 under **Enabling Device Location**.

Displaying Maps & Getting Directions

You can use the Windows Maps app included with Windows to display locations on a map anywhere in the world and to get directions from one location to another. As discussed previously, Maps works by using the location data available to Windows and relies on this information to be available. That said, you can set a default location to use when location information isn't available and you can always map directions between two points on a map.

To display a location:

1. Type **Maps** in the Search box.

> **TIP**: If the Search box isn't displayed on the taskbar, click **Start** and then type **Maps** in the Search box.

2. Click **Maps** in the search results. Maps should be listed as a Trusted Windows Store App and the Best Match.
3. If this is the first time you've started Maps, the app asks if it can use your location information. Click **Yes**.

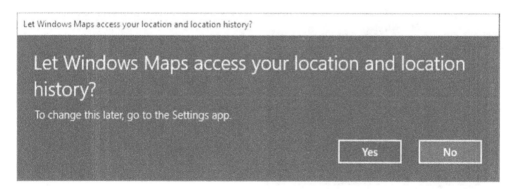

4. Type a street address or the name of a location into Maps.
5. Select the location in the search results.

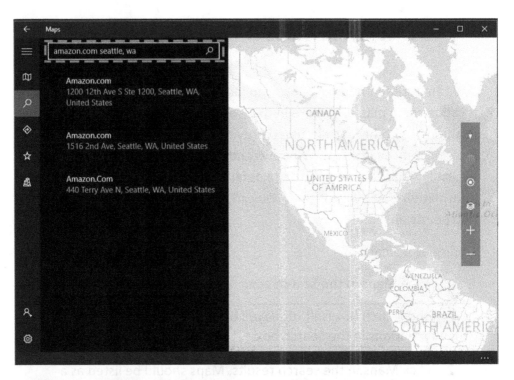

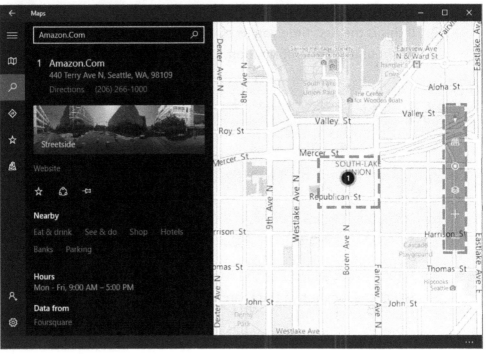

Maps provides information about the location and also displays the location on the map. Use the map options to control the view:

 Rotates map so north is up.

 Tilts the view between map view and street level view.

 Shows your location on the map.

 Displays view selections. Choose Aerial, Traffic or a Street-side view.

 Zooms in (so does CTRL + +)

 Zooms out (so does CTRL + -)

Maps also makes it simple to get directions from one place to another. You specify the starting point and destination for a trip and then Maps provides directions for getting there by driving, transit or walking.

To get directions:

1. Click **Directions** (   ).
2. Click the travel method:

 Car

 Transit

 Walking

3. Type the name or address of the location where you will start your trip.

TIP: Maps uses your current location as the default start location. If that's true, you don't need to enter a start location.

---

4. Type the name or address of the location where you will end your trip, then press **Enter**.
5. Maps displays an overview of the route and tells you how long the trip will take. For car and transit trips, the trip time is adjusted based on current traffic levels.

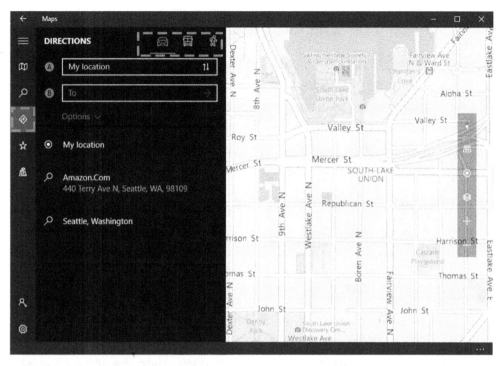

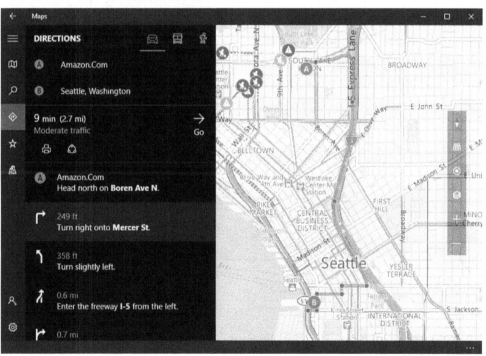

Checking Your Weather

Much as Windows Maps uses location data to provide directions and information, the Weather app can use location data to provide information about weather at your location. The Weather app gets its weather information from the MSN Weather service provided by Microsoft.

To check your weather for the first time:

1. Type **Weather** in the Search box.

> **TIP**: If the Search box isn't displayed on the taskbar, click **Start** and then type **Weather** in the Search box.

2. Click **Weather** in the search results. Weather should be listed as a Trusted Windows Store App and the Best Match.
3. If this is the first time you've started Weather, the app asks you to set the default location.
4. Click **Fahrenheit** or **Celsius**.
5. Type the name of the default location, such as **Seattle, WA**.
6. When you see the location you want to use in the list, click it.
7. The Weather app then displays the current conditions and a forecast for the default location.

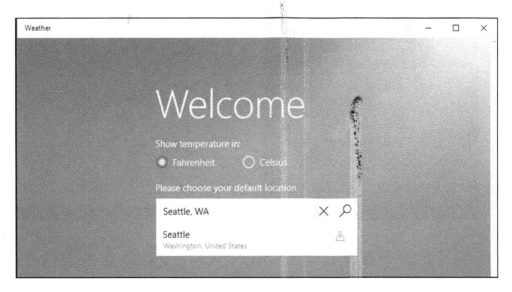

To check the weather in another location:

1. Start the Weather app.
2. Type the name of the location in the Weather app's Search box.
3. When you see the location you want to use in the list, click it.
4. The Weather app then displays the current conditions and a forecast for the specified location.

Instead of getting weather for the default location, you can configure the Weather app to always use location data to get updated weather information for whatever location you are currently at.

To use your current location for weather:

1. Start the Weather app.

2. Click the Weather app's **Settings** (　) button.

3. Under Launch Location, click **Always Detect My Location**.

4. Click **Back** ().

5. The Weather app then displays the current conditions and a forecast for your current location.

Getting Current News & Events

News is another app that can use location information to customize what you see whenever you are using the app. By default, News displays national and world news. The News app gets its headlines and events from the MSN News service provided by Microsoft.

To get the latest news:

1. Type **News** in the Search box.

TIP: If the Search box isn't displayed on the taskbar, click **Start** and then type **News** in the Search box.

---

2. Click **News** in the search results. News should be listed as a Trusted Windows Store App and the Best Match.
3. The News app then displays current headlines from around the country and around the world.
4. Click a category to get news for that category.

Instead of getting national and world news, you can configure the News app to use location data to get local news for whatever location you are currently at.

To have the News app always use your current location for local news:

1. Start the News app.

2. Click the **Local** ( ) button.

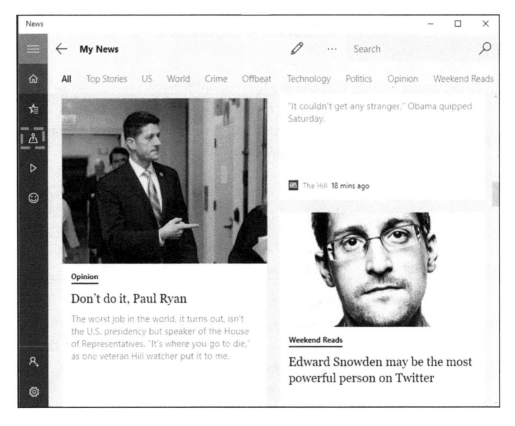

3. If you haven't configured location data yet for News, the apps requests access to location data. Click **Yes**.

4. The News app then displays local news whenever you click the Local () button.

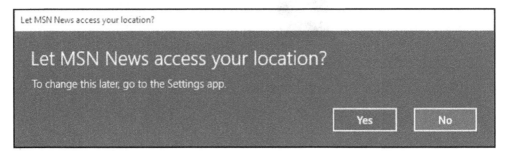

The News app provides options for streamlining the news and only getting information about areas of interest, such as Top Stories, Technology, Politics and Opinion but not Entertainment or Money.

To streamline the news:

1. Start the News app.
2. Click the **Interests** ( ) button.
3. Areas of interest for which you are currently getting news are shown with a checkmark on a green circle.
4. If you don't want news for a particular area of interest, click the **Selected** ( ) button to clear the selection.
5. If you want news for a particular area of interest, click the **Add** ( ) button to select it.

Uninstalling Apps

If you don't use an app, you should uninstall it. This will free up disk space and ensure that Windows doesn't keep downloading and installing updates for an app that you don't even use.

The way you uninstall an app depends on whether it is a universal app or traditional software. You can uninstall universal apps via Start and the All Apps list. You uninstall traditional software using Programs And Features.

To uninstall a universal app pinned to Start:

1. Click **Start** ( ) to display the Start menu.
2. Right-click the app on the Start menu.
3. Click **Uninstall**.

To uninstall a universal app via the All Apps list:

1. Click **Start** ( ) to display the Start menu.
2. Click **All Apps** ( ) to display the All Apps sidebar.
3. Right-click the App and then click **Uninstall**.

Windows provides several other options for uninstalling universal apps, including options that help you find apps by name, space used and installation date.

To locate and then uninstall apps by name, size or install date:

1. Click **Start** (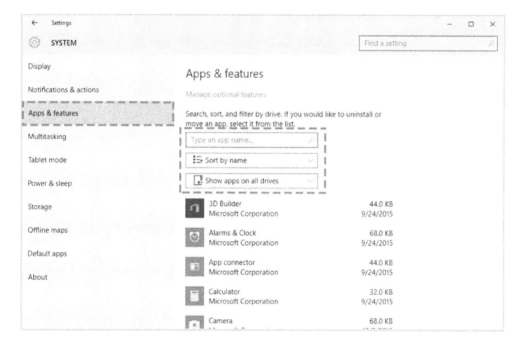) to display the Start menu.

2. Click **Settings** ( ) to open the Settings app.
3. Click **System** and then click **Apps & Features**.

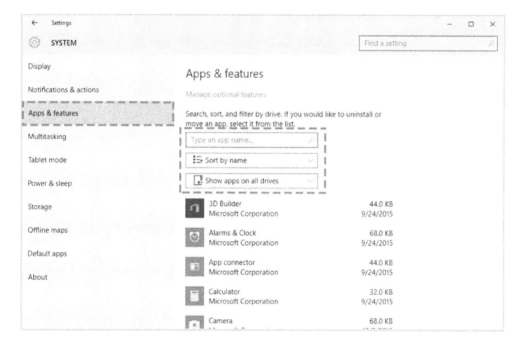

4. To find an app by name, type the app name in the text box provided.
5. Use the Sort selection list to sort apps by name, size or install date.
6. Click the App and then click **Uninstall**.

Uninstalling Packaged Software

Most traditional software uses a Setup program for installation and this program also helps manage the removal process.

To uninstall traditional software:

1. Type **uninstall** in the Search box.

> **TIP**: If the Search box isn't displayed on the taskbar, click **Start** and then type **uninstall** in the Search box.

2. In the search results, click **Change Or Remove A Program** to open the Programs And Features page in Control Panel.
3. Click the program that you want to uninstall.

4. Click **Uninstall** (or **Uninstall/Change**).
5. Follow the prompts (which are different for various types of programs).

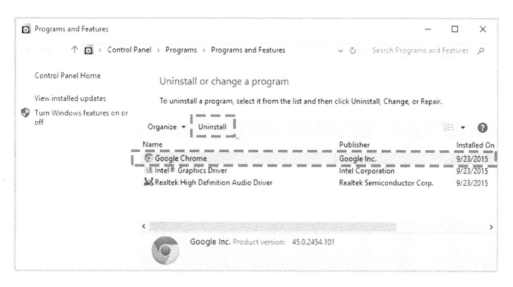

Day 7

Customizing Windows & Your Environment

Day 7.
Customizing Windows & Your Environment

Lesson Notes: In Day 7, you learn how to customize Windows and paint the virtual walls with your personal colors, backgrounds and pictures. You also learn how to adjust basic settings and customize your account.

Windows provides a virtual space for you to work, so why not customize it like you would customize your room, home or apartment? Areas of the operating system you can personalize include your account picture, the desktop background, windows colors, and lock screen.

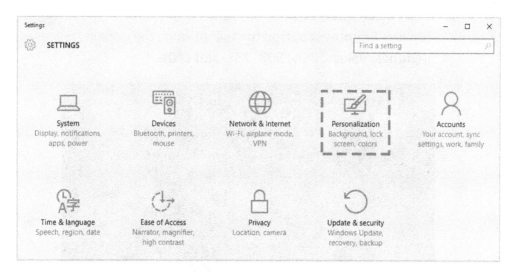

Adjusting Brightness & Volume

When you are using a laptop, tablet or smart phone, you'll often need to adjust the brightness to accommodate the current circumstances. For example, when you are outside, you often need to turn the brightness to a higher setting than when you are indoors. As your screen uses a lot of power, you may also want to adjust the brightness to extend the battery life of your device. In contrast, when your device is plugged in and running on AC power, battery life isn't an issue.

To adjust screen brightness:

1. Click **Power** ().
2. Click the **Brightness** button to cycle through the default brightness values: 25%, 50%, 75% and 100%.

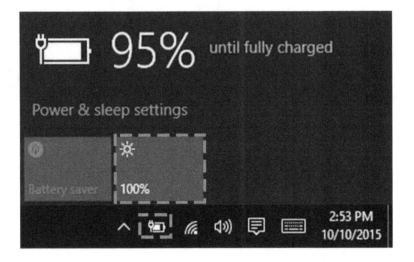

When you are listening to music, watching a movie or playing a game, you'll often need to adjust the volume up or down. If you are by yourself, you may be able to have the volume on a higher setting than if others are around you. Sometimes, you also may need to mute the sound temporarily.

To adjust the volume:

1. Click **Volume** ( ) on the taskbar.
2. Click and drag the Volume slider to set the volume level. Drag to the left to lower the volume. Drag to the right to raise the volume.

To mute the volume:

1. Click **Volume** ( ) on the taskbar.
2. Click the **Mute** button in the notification panel to change

 to .

To unmute the sound:

1. Click **Volume** () on the taskbar.
2. Drag the Volume slider, or click the Mute button to change 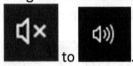 to .

Changing the Desktop Background

The desktop background can display a solid color, a picture or a slideshow.

To use a solid color for the desktop background:

1. Right-click an open area of the desktop, then select **Personalize**. This opens the Personalize page in the Settings app.
2. Click **Background**.
3. Click the **Background** list, then select **Solid Color**.
4. Click the color you want to use.

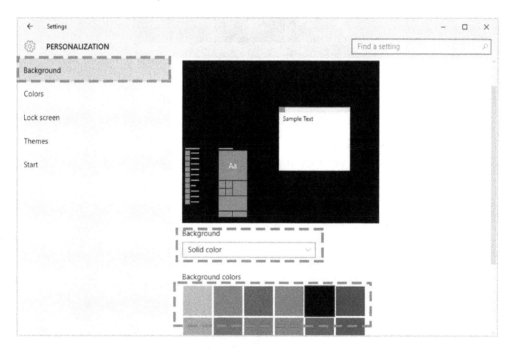

To use a picture for the desktop background:

1. Right-click an open area of the desktop, then select **Personalize**. This opens the Personalize page in the Settings app.
2. Click **Background**.

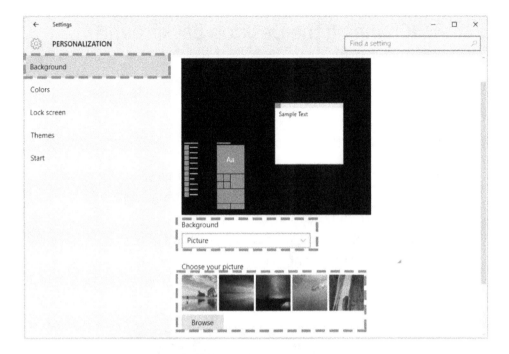

3. Click the **Background** list, then select **Picture**.
4. To use a default image, click the picture you want to use and skip the remaining steps.
5. To use one of your own pictures, click **Browse**.

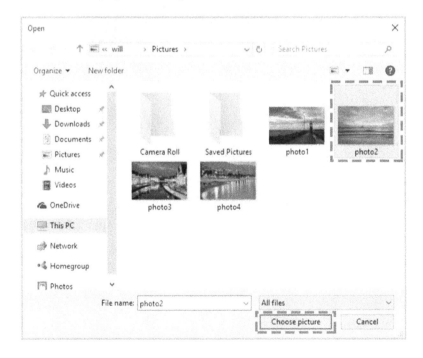

6. Click the picture that you want to use.
7. Click **Choose Picture**.

To use a picture slideshow on the desktop background:

1. Right-click an open area of the desktop, then select **Personalize**. This opens the Personalize page in the Settings app.
2. Click **Background**.
3. Click the **Background** list, then select **Slideshow**.

By default, your Pictures library is used as the source for the slide show. To remove the Picture folder or any other you add later, click the folder then click **Remove**.

To add a folder to use as a source for the slideshow:

1. Click **Add A Folder**.
2. Click the folder that you want to use.
3. Click **Choose This Folder**.

Modifying Accent Colors & Transparency

By default, Windows chooses accent colors for window borders and highlights based on the colors used in the desktop background you choose but doesn't show the accent color on Start, the taskbar, or Action Center. Windows also makes the backgrounds for Start, taskbar and Action Center transparent (which many users find distracting).

To modify the way accent colors and transparency are used:

1. Right-click an open area of the desktop, then select **Personalize**. This opens the Personalize page in the Settings app.
2. Click **Colors**.
3. To have Windows pick an accent color from your background, click the **Automatically Pick An Accent Color...** switch to **On**. Otherwise, click the switch to **Off**, then click the accent color to use.
4. To have Windows show the accent color on Start, the taskbar and Action Center, click the **Show Color...** switch to **On**.
5. To have remove transparency from Start, the taskbar and Action Center, click the **Make Start, Taskbar...** switch to **Off**.

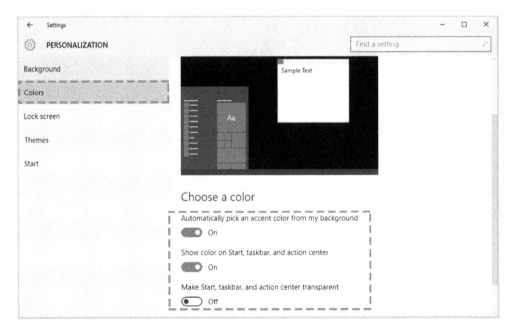

Changing the Lock Screen Background

You can personalize the lock screen by changing the picture that is displayed in the background or using a picture slideshow.

To change the lock screen picture:

1. Right-click an open area of the desktop, then select **Personalize**. This opens the Personalize page in the Settings app.
2. Click **Lock Screen**.
3. Click the **Background** list, then select **Picture**.
4. To use a default image, click the picture you want to use and skip the remaining steps.
5. To use one of your own pictures, click **Browse**.
6. Click the picture that you want to use.
7. Click **Choose Picture**.

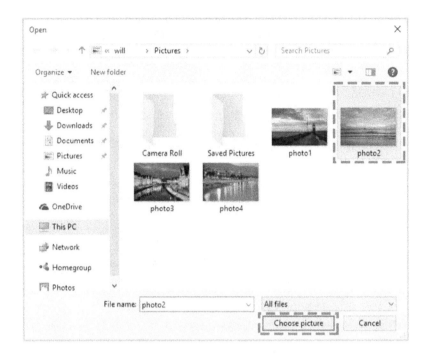

To use a picture slideshow on the lock screen:

1. Right-click an open area of the desktop, then select **Personalize**. This opens the Personalize page in the Settings app.
2. Click **Lock Screen**.
3. Click the **Background** list, then select **Slideshow**.

By default, your Pictures library is used as the source for the slide show. To remove the Picture folder or any other you add later, click the folder then click **Remove**.

To add a folder to use as a source for the slideshow:

1. Click **Add A Folder**.
2. Click the folder that you want to use.
3. Click **Choose This Folder**.

Changing Your Account Picture

The default account picture Windows displays on Start and the Lock screen is okay but nothing fancy:

You can personalize Windows by changing this account picture to something more interesting, like a picture of you, your car or your pet. You also can take a picture using the camera on your device.

To use a personal photo as your account picture:

1. Click **Start** () to display the Start menu.

2. Click **Settings** () to open the Settings app.
3. Click **Accounts**, then click **Your Account**.
4. To use one of your own pictures, click **Browse**.

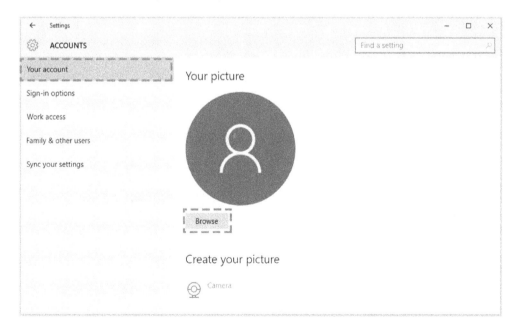

5. Click the picture that you want to use.
6. Click **Choose Picture**.

To take a picture using the device camera and use this as your account picture:

1. Click **Start** () to display the Start menu.

2. Click **Settings** () to open the Settings app.
3. Click **Accounts**, then click **Your Account**.
4. Click **Camera**.

Managing Your Password

Your user account should have a password and you should change the password periodically. Another reason to change your password is if you find it difficult to remember your password or someone else has learned your password.

The way you change your password depends on whether you have a local user account or a Microsoft account.

To change the password of a local user account:

1. Click **Start** ( ) to display the Start menu.

TIP: To change another user's password, sign in as that user.

2. Click **Settings** ( ) to open the Settings app.
3. Click **Accounts**, then click **Sign-in Options**.
4. Under the **Password** heading, click **Change**.

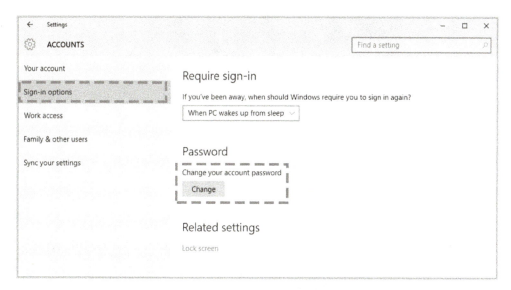

> **TIP**: If your account doesn't have a password, click **Add** under the
> **Password** heading and skip step 5.

1. Type your current password, then click **Next**.
2. Type and then retype your new password.
3. Type a password hint.
4. Click **Next** and then click **Finish**.
5. Use the new password the next time you sign in with this local account.

To change the password of a Microsoft account:

1. Click **Start** (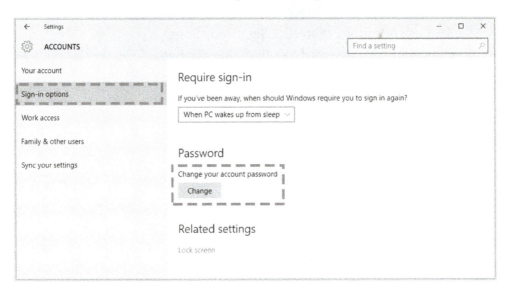) to display the Start menu.
2. Click **Settings** ( ) to open the Settings app.
3. Click **Accounts**, then click **Sign-in Options**.
4. Under the **Password** heading, click **Change**.

← Settings		− □ ×
⚙ **ACCOUNTS**		Find a setting 🔍
Your account	**Require sign-in**	
Sign-in options	If you've been away, when should Windows require you to sign in again?	
Work access	When PC wakes up from sleep ∨	
Family & other users	**Password**	
Sync your settings	Change your account password	
	Change	
	Related settings	
	Lock screen	

5. If you aren't currently signed in to your Microsoft account, type your password, then click **Sign In**.
6. Type your current password.
7. Type and then retype your new password.

8. Click **Next** and then click **Finish**.

If you try to access Microsoft account features, you may see a prompt stating your credentials aren't current. If so, you'll need to sign-in using your new password when prompted. Be sure to use your new password the next time you sign in with your Microsoft account as well.

> **TIP**: While you are working with Accounts in the Settings app, you may want to view or manage the related settings that are stored in the profile by Microsoft. If so, click **Your Account** and then click **Manage My Microsoft Account**.

Managing Other User Accounts

If you want to share your device with someone else, you can add a user account for that person. As all user accounts are separate from each other, the new user account will have its own settings, apps, documents and more.

You can create additional user accounts as local user accounts or Microsoft accounts. Users can be added as family members or simply as additional users. If you have children and want to be able to control their access to websites, apps and games or set time limits, you should create a family account. Otherwise, you'll probably want to create an additional user, which doesn't have restrictions or limits.

To create a user account:

1. Click **Start** (   ) to display the Start menu.

2. Click **Settings** (   ) to open the Settings app.
3. Click **Accounts**, then click **Family & Other Users**.

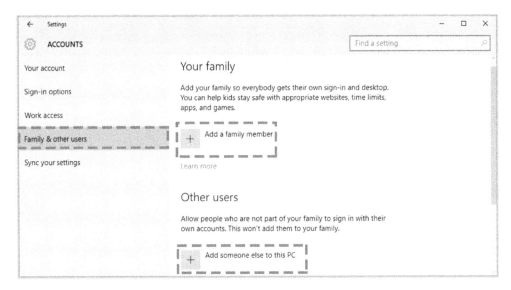

4. To create an account for a family member, click **Add A Family Member**. When prompted specify whether you are adding a child or adult by clicking either **Add A Child** or **Add An Adult**.
5. To create an account for an additional user, click **Add Someone Else To This PC**.

- If the user has an existing Microsoft account, you can connect to it as discussed in **Connecting a New User to an Existing Account**.
- Otherwise, you need to create a new Microsoft account and connect it to the user's account as discussed in **Configuring a New Account for a User**.

Connecting a New User to an Existing Account

After following Steps 1-5 under **Managing Other User Accounts**, connect the user to an existing Microsoft account by following these steps:

1. Type the email address associated with the Microsoft account, such as bob.roberts.training@gmail.com.
2. Click **Next**.
3. Click **Confirm** (or click **Finish** if you are adding an additional user).
4. Windows lets you know that for the user to login the first time, the device will need to be connected to the Internet.

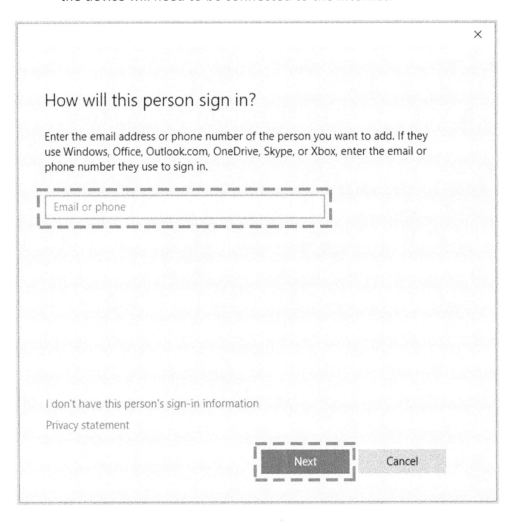

Windows connects the Microsoft account to your device. When the user logs in, he or she will need to use their Microsoft account email address and the password for their Microsoft account.

> **TIP**: Don't forget the user will still need to verify his or her identity on your Windows device. See **Verifying Your Account**.

Configuring a New Account for a User

After following Steps 1-5 under **Managing Other User Accounts**, connect the user to a new Microsoft account by following these steps:

1. When prompted to confirm how this person will sign in, click **I Don't Have This Person's Sign-In Information**. Or if you are adding a family member account, click **The Person I Want To Add Doesn't Have An Email Address**.

Let's create your account

Windows, Office, Outlook.com, OneDrive, Skype, Xbox. They're all better and more personal when you sign in with your Microsoft account.* Learn more

| First name | Last name |

someone@example.com

Get a new email address

Password

United States

| Birth month | Day | Year |

*If you already use a Microsoft service, go Back to sign in with that account.

Next   Back

2. Type the user's first and last name.
3. Specify the email address you want to use. If you have an email account that you want to use, enter this email address and proceed to the next step. Otherwise, click **Get A New Email Address**. Next, type the user name you want to use with Outlook. Your new email address will be *username*@outlook.com.

> **NOTE**: When creating an account for a family member, Microsoft assumes the user needs a new email address, so your first option is to type the user name you want to use with Outlook. If the family member has an email address, click **Use Their Email Address Instead**. You'll then be able to enter an email address to use.

4. Type the password you want to use with this Microsoft account.
5. Select the country.
6. Specify the date of birth.
7. Click **Next**.

You next need to provide additional security information so if the user ever forgets his or her password Microsoft can send a text message to help the user reset the password. If the user doesn't have a mobile phone, you can provide Microsoft with an alternative email address instead and then this email address will be used verifying the user's identity if he or she ever forgets their password.

1. If you want to associate a mobile phone number with your account. Select your phone number's country code and then type your mobile phone number. Click **Next**.
2. If you want to associate an alternative email address with your account instead of a mobile phone number, click **Add An Alternate Email Instead**. Type the alternate email address and then click **Next**.
3. Choose an option when Windows asks how you want to receive your security code to verify your account and then click **Next**.
4. Specify whether you want the user to have an enhanced online experience and get offers from Microsoft.
5. Click **Next**.
6. Click **Close**.
7. That's it, you're done!

Windows connects the Microsoft account to your device. When the user logs in, he or she will need to use their Microsoft account email address and the password for their Microsoft account.

> **TIP**: Don't forget the user will still need to verify his or her identity on your Windows device. See **Verifying Your Account**.

Deleting a User Account

If you have a user account that is no longer needed or an account for someone who should no longer be able to sign in to your device, you can delete the user account. When you delete a user account, the account is no longer available on the device and there won't be sign in options on the Lock screen for the user. Windows also removes the user's settings, documents and other data stored on the device, which frees up disk space.

To delete a user account:

1. Click **Start** (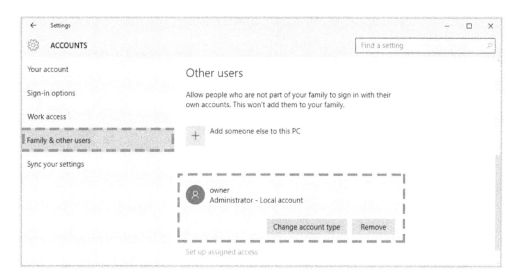) to display the Start menu.
2. Click **Settings** ( ) to open the Settings app.
3. Click **Accounts**, then click **Family & Other Users**.
4. Click the user account that you want to delete to select it.
5. Click **Remove**.

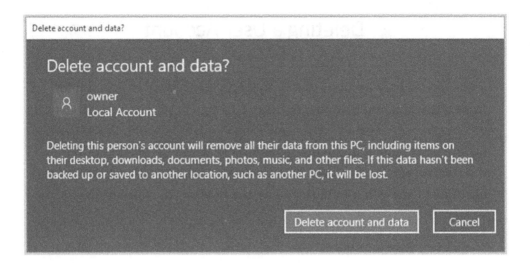

Delete account and data?

Delete account and data?

👤 owner
Local Account

Deleting this person's account will remove all their data from this PC, including items on their desktop, downloads, documents, photos, music, and other files. If this data hasn't been backed up or saved to another location, such as another PC, it will be lost.

| Delete account and data | Cancel |

6. When prompted to confirm that you want to delete the user's account and all associated data, click **Delete Account and Data**.
7. Windows deletes the account and removes all settings, documents and other data for this account.

Where to Next...

Now that you've learned how to perform many essential tasks with Windows 10, you're ready to begin using the operating system in your everyday life. Should you have additional questions, don't forget that this book is designed to be used as a reference too.

If you need to have the book open while you work, that's okay! Just open to the section that discusses the task you want to perform and follow along.

Before you close the book and call it a day, why don't you stop by the Store and see if there are any new apps, games, albums, TV shows or movies that catch your eye!

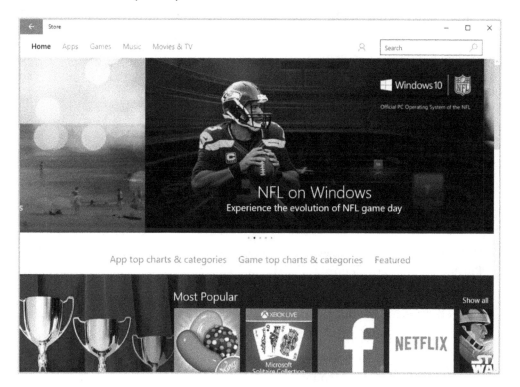

Lessons In Review

Notes

Notes

Notes

Notes

Thank you...

Thank you for purchasing *Learn Windows 10 in 1 Quick Week*. Please support this book if you found it to be useful. I hope to write other books and your support will help me do that!

www.ingramcontent.com/pod-product-compliance
Lightning Source LLC
Chambersburg PA
CBHW080413060326
40689CB00019B/4227